THE GOOD FORK COOKBOOK

THE GOOD FORK COOKBOOK

SOHUI KIM

WITH RACHEL WHARTON

FOREWORD BY ANDREW KNOWLTON
PHOTOGRAPHY BY BURCU AVSAR AND ZACH DESART

ABRAMS, NEW YORK

DEDICATED TO

the greatest Buena Forchettas:

Jane and Peter Schneider;

my father,

Dae Sik Kim;

and my two amazing children,

Jasper and Oliver,

who will hopefully one day

cook these recipes

while I sit in the backyard

and drink a glass of wine.

Contents

Foreword
====

YOU KNOW THE KIND OF PEOPLE WHO MAKE YOU MAD because you wish you could be like them? That's who Sohui Kim and Ben Schneider are to me.

It all began in 2003 over a plate of grilled chicken thighs. My friend St. John Frizell, who was a copy editor at *Bon Appétit* at the time, had just moved into a ground-floor rental in Red Hook, Brooklyn, a quiet waterfront hamlet that felt thousands of miles away from the hustle of New York City. The apartment was a shoebox, but it had a big backyard, and St. John was smart enough to see its party potential. His new landlords needed help cleaning it up, and I volunteered. Beer and food were promised and, at the age we were, that's all it took to get a dozen or so people to pitch in. As the sun began to set, the landlords, Sohui and Ben, rolled out a keg of Brooklyn Lager and set out a platter of chicken thighs.

The chicken had been marinated in soy sauce, ginger, garlic, honey, and gochujang and then charred on a Weber. It was spicy—perfectly tender on the inside, and impossibly crunchy on the outside. I realized at that moment that I wasn't as good a cook as I had thought. Sohui probably doesn't even remember cooking that meal—it was something she had simply thrown together at the last minute. As I would later learn, that's what she does. She makes people happy with food.

Over the next two years, that backyard became my life. There was party after party. There were *pétanque* tournaments, weddings, and bonfires set in old oil drums around which we would recap our workweeks and drink and smoke too much. There were plays—real plays with actors and scripts and costumes and props—and people paid to watch them. I became the unofficial backyard bartender, behind the bar Ben had built one weekend. That backyard wasn't just a gathering place; it was the grange hall of the Red Hook community. It's where, you could say, I became an adult. Everyone who spent time there was lucky, and we all had Sohui and Ben to thank.

But they also made me envious. Ben could drink more beer than I could—and not fall down. He could build anything: a house, a float for Coney Island's annual Mermaid Parade, a Broadway-worthy stage. Give him a box of toothpicks and a tube of Krazy Glue, and the next day you'd have a boat to take you to nearby Liberty Island. His beard was always better than mine, and he even owned a pickup truck—in New York City!

Sohui introduced me to the world of Korean cooking with its fire and funk. She taught me how to cook rice with my instincts—the ultimate gift, in my book. Plus, she did it all with a big smile and an even bigger heart. I think she could drink more than I could, too.

Soon, they told me they were thinking of opening a restaurant around the corner from their house. As someone who has seen great restaurants come and go, I attempted to talk them out of it. It was too hard, I said. Too time-consuming, too thankless. But I was simply being selfish. What would happen to our backyard parties? What would I do with all my weekends? Where would I drink kegs of cold Schaefer beer, listen to Willie's Roadhouse on Sirius XM, and just shoot the shit?

Thankfully for Red Hook and New York and, yes, me, they didn't listen. After ten years, The Good Fork is better than ever. It's not just the place where you go to eat Sohui's famous Korean-style Steak and Eggs (page 94) or drink a cold beer with Ben while you ask him, again, how he built the place all by himself. It's not just a place where I go to see old friends and meet new ones. It's not just a restaurant in Red Hook; it *is* Red Hook.

I still hold a grudge against Sohui and Ben for being better than me at pretty much everything. But now, thanks to the book you are holding, I can at least try to cook like them.

ANDREW KNOWLTON, 2016

WHEN MY HUSBAND, BEN, AND I OPENED THE GOOD FORK in March 2006—in a far-flung corner of New York City two miles from the nearest subway station—we had no publicist, no corporate advisors, no money left in the bank, and only a vague idea of how to run a restaurant. I had been cooking in professional kitchens for many years, but I hadn't run one on my own yet. And Ben, a carpenter and actor, thought he could host, bartend, and manage at the same time, without any experience doing any of those things. The result was a guy in a nice shirt going around in circles and accomplishing none of those tasks. What we did have was a passion for food, and I had a unique approach to cooking it. Our opening menu didn't follow any trend or particular style. It was a collection of ideas and flavors that made their way from my early childhood in Korea to my upbringing in the Bronx to my time in some of the finest kitchens of New York to the plate and into our bellies. It might not have been proper Korean or French or American or Italian, but it tasted really good, and it was what Ben and I liked to eat. A style emerged: traditional dishes heightened by a global pantry; classics, with just enough of a twist to make them new again.

I knew well before we opened The Good Fork that I wanted to cook globally inspired cuisine, not exotic or eclectic—just flavorful. It's how I cooked at home: I would add a dab of Chinese fermented black beans to my gravy when I roasted a chicken (a trick I learned from Anita Lo), or kimchee to my steak and eggs. Ultimately I merged everything I'd learned about French and Italian technique from my day job as a cook with the American classics I'd come to love and the Korean cooking that's in my bones. I was using whatever ingredients I saw at the market or the local farm stand that looked fresh and good and exciting. Most of my friends and family told me I was crazy to put Asian dumplings and wild boar ragu on the same menu. But I knew it could work. Even though a lot of what I do seems like common sense now, playing around with culinary traditions and blending borders wasn't the norm at that time, even in New York.

But my life hadn't been the norm, either. I left Korea when I was ten, and I still have strong memories of that time, many dreamlike, and most of them involving food. It was another world. I remember street food, from rice cakes to periwinkles, my free-spirited mother practicing fine French pastry and Korean royal court cuisine that she learned in cooking classes, and my Buddhist/Shaman grandmother soaking tree bark, foraging for edible weeds in the mountains, and fermenting kimchee in our backyard.

My name was given to me by a Buddhist monk: It means "peaceful pond." The "So" part of my name—meaning "small pond"—replenishes the natural element of water my astrological sign dangerously lacks, according to my grandmother. Her solution was to add it to my name, so I can live a full and balanced life. "Hui," on the other hand, means "hopeful" or "peaceful." Her dictum was, "Sohui-ya, you must settle down and live near water to be truly happy." So living in Red Hook, which is surrounded by water, was destiny. Thank Buddha!

Despite all the deliciousness that surrounded me at home and at many extended family gatherings, I was a very picky eater as a small child. You could not get me to eat kimchee unless there was a big bowl of water on the table so I could wash off the pepper paste. This memory isn't lost on me as I try to raise two very picky eaters of my own. In fact, back then I ate so many eggs over plain steamed rice, they used to call me "the egg monster" (*kaeran kyushin*).

When my father moved us to America in 1981, to the Bronx neighborhood of Parkchester in New York City, my brother and I went crazy over pizza and hamburgers, which seemed so foreign to us. We each gained ten pounds during our first year here! Like many other Koreans in New York City, Dad opened a produce market with the help of a collective formed by other Korean immigrants—though he had once run a successful construction company in Korea, he arrived in the States with only $2,000 to his name taped to his stomach under his shirt. Working with him at the market, I learned about all kinds of fruits and vegetables I had never seen before. Sunday was our one day off, and we would often go to the waterfront neighborhood called City Island for lobsters, barbecue my Dad's L.A.-style kalbi beef with other Korean families at picnics in Connecticut, or go to Hop Kee in Manhattan's Chinatown and eat chow fun and Cantonese snails with brown sauce.

In high school, I received a scholarship for "academically talented" inner-city kids for a school in Darien, Connecticut. It was just forty-five minutes from the Bronx, but it was another world. I lived in a boarding house with Latinas,

African Americans, and other Asians, all of us from the city. We were the only minorities or students of color in the school. One of the best parts of this truly odd high school experience was our part-time cook, Effie, a heavyset Southerner. I was fascinated by her food and would take notes while she made dinner: I would watch her fry chicken in Crisco, or make super-rich macaroni and cheese and big trays of cornbread. It was a huge deal to me—I'd only had fried chicken that came in a paper bucket before that, and Korean fried chicken wasn't invented yet.

Then, when I went to Bowdoin College in Maine, there was lots of instant ramen and beer. So I learned how to cook for myself and started making French toast, baked chicken, and quick bread from my *Better Homes & Gardens* cookbook—the one covered in red gingham—while dreaming about writing a cookbook one day titled *One Hundred and One Ways to Cook with Instant Ramen*. I only lasted two years in Maine because I missed New York City, so I finished up my liberal arts degree at Barnard College. I lived in a dorm with seven other women in upper Manhattan, spending my free time searching out the city's secret $5 meals and best falafel. Once I graduated, I got a job at an architectural publishing company—and lucky for me, my boss, Kazumi, happened to be a food lover. She often took me out to places like the Odeon, Teddy's, and Omen, all great New York restaurants at the time.

By this point, I'd moved to Brooklyn and had my first real kitchen, equipped with the copy of *Joy of Cooking* my sister had bought me and *The Fanny Farmer Cookbook* I'd bought myself. I would hit this fantastic Polish market in my neighborhood, the Korean groceries like my Dad's, and the Brooklyn Chinatown a few blocks north. I hosted many dinner parties in my small apartment.

Nobody else I knew cooked, and my friends started telling me I should open a restaurant or catering business. Maybe it was my Korean immigrant upbringing: I believed that food was very important, but it was not what you pursued as a profession, just an interest to pursue as a hobby. But after a decade intending to chase my late father's dream that I become a lawyer, I realized there was a reason I still hadn't yet finished those applications to law school. I didn't want to go…and it only took twenty-nine years to realize it. Instead, I applied to the Peter Kump's New York Cooking School (now known as the Institute of Culinary Education) in Manhattan.

The moment I got to culinary school, I knew I'd made the right choice. After I finished, I gravitated toward what I call "thinking chefs," and not pan-throwing chefs. I got an externship with chefs Dan Barber and Michael Anthony at Blue Hill restaurant, and I stayed there working for free doing pastry until they offered me a job at Dan's new place up in Westchester, Blue Hill at Stone Barns. But I wanted to stay in the city, and so Michael got me a job instead with Anita Lo, who had opened Annisa down the street. There, I was a sponge. I felt the creativity in me for the first time, and I wanted to run with it.

When I got to Annisa, I immediately felt like it was more my speed. Anita is a fantastic chef doing her own fine dining thing, and the kitchen was all women. We would shoot the shit and work our asses off. I formed some of the strongest bonds in that kitchen. It was fun, and I got my butt kicked; it was the first job that I ever lost sleep over. I would pray for a slow night just so I could catch up. But after a year and a half, I had worked my way through the stations and knew how to be a pretty darn good line cook, so I figured that to learn more I had to move on.

Over the next couple of years I worked to fill in what I saw as holes in my skills: I butchered pigs to make salamis with Food Network star Anne Burrell when she still ran the kitchen of Mario Batali's Italian Wine Merchants. I tested pasta after pasta recipe for Cesare Casella, one of the country's finest Italian chefs. And I worked the executive dining room at Sony, where Chef Morimoto got his start making sushi. It was no-holds-barred in terms of what we cooked for those executives. I learned sushi, I made pizza, and I prepared formal French sauces day after day.

By then I had been working in restaurants for six years, and I felt—cockily, of course—that I knew what I was doing, even though in retrospect I really didn't yet know that much. I was living in Brooklyn in Red Hook with my husband, Ben, who is a woodworker and an actor. We met in 2001, when my best friend from the Bronx, Okwui, was appearing in a small production of Jean Cocteau's *Orphée*. Ben was in the show with Okwui, and like me, he geeked out on food. His parents were Upper West Side anthropologists who studied Sicilian culture and the Mafia—he'd even lived in Italy as a little kid. On one of our first dates he greeted me with oysters on the half shell—and he even had an old ice crusher to prepare a bed of ice to display them on. Then he made me his mother's osso buco and risotto. (He hasn't made it since, but I remember it was really, really good.)

We still live in Red Hook. The neighborhood is right on the waterfront, cut off from the rest of Brooklyn by an eight-lane highway. Many who used to live in the East Village, Chelsea, or Williamsburg and just wanted to be left alone to do their thing eventually came here. They settled right in alongside the old-timers, the guys who used to work the ships when this was one of the country's biggest working ports. There were still packs of wild dogs roaming the streets when we moved there. Somebody was building a farm on a basketball court around the corner where we now buy some of our greens, and someone else was starting a brewery where we now get some of our beers. There was—and sometimes still is—the sense that anything goes, and also that you can do anything there.

At home in Red Hook on weekends, we would have big barbecues, weddings, cooking parties, or crazy, artsy backyard plays led by Ben and our friends Linden and St. John. I would make homey, comforting food that was a blend of all my experiences: dozens of pork-filled fried dumplings that were a little bit Korean and a little bit Chinese, whole pigs cooked in a roasting box in our backyard, steak and eggs with funky kimchee, or homemade pastas with real Italian ragu. It was influenced by everything I knew, everything I had tasted, and everything I liked.

Then, I came home from work one day and Ben said to me, "I found our spot." He was as great a builder as an actor, and he was always looking for a project. We went right down and looked at the space, just around the corner from our house, and I knew this was it. We had never seriously talked about our own place before that. Ben had been telling me forever that I needed my own restaurant, and I had dreamed of being the chef of my own place someday. But I hadn't thought it would happen so soon. We didn't have a penny in the bank, but we borrowed some money from my amazingly supportive in-laws, Peter and Jane, to make a restaurant, on the cheap. Our whole business plan was that Ben would build it using his woodworking know-how, and that I would cook the food I'd been making for friends at home, and somehow fill in the blanks along the way. What better way to combine our interests?

We built the restaurant ourselves, and Peter helped us name it The Good Fork, a riff on the Italian slang *la buona forchetta*, which in Italy is what they call a

chowhound, or someone who loves to eat. Without any announcements or press, we opened, making a menu we weren't sure how to explain. "Sohui, what are you doing?" I remember my brother saying. "You can't put wild boar ragu and pork dumplings on the same menu. That's stupid." (That's tough love.) I figured worse-case scenario it would last six months, and then I'd go get a job at another restaurant.

Instead, all our seats filled with family and friends the first night, then again the next night with more people we didn't know, and they just kept filling up. The fourth week, the *New York Times* came. We weren't ready, but Peter Meehan gave us a good review. Soon we were turning our tables two or three times a night. By summer the *New Yorker* and *GQ* wrote about us, and the James Beard House called. I won a Food Network *Throwdown with Bobby Flay* making dumplings, and we had to hire another cook and a bartender. The Good Fork and Red Hook were on the rise. That summer, *Time Out New York* declared on its cover, "Red Hook Has Arrived!"

Ten years later, we are no longer the next big thing in the coolest new neighborhood, and at least three books have been written about the new Brooklyn food scene. We appear in all of them, but more importantly, we're still here, better than ever.

Our restaurant feels like a family—not just our regulars, but our staff, servers, and cooks, many of whom have been here almost as long as we have. They have contributed not just with their hard work, but also with recipes and new ideas. There are the traditional Mexican salsas we learned from our sous-chef, who learned them from his mother. There are the soba and ramen recipes we've learned in order to host Noodle Night, something I started for the Red Hook regulars who come in every week.

Recently, there are the growing number of traditional Korean dishes I am now making a point to rediscover, or learn for the first time, trying them at home for our children, and then adding them to our repertoire at the restaurant. We opened Insa, our second restaurant in an up-and-coming neighborhood called Gowanus, not far from our home. This time, we're dedicating the place to traditional Korean cooking.

Insa, just like The Good Fork, was handcrafted, designed, and built by Ben with a skeleton crew of capable builders and craftsmen. And just like The Good

Fork, the design was thought up only after we signed the lease to 4,600 square feet of empty, raw space. Luckily, Ben and I walked in and almost immediately imagined where the kitchen would be, could feel the warmth of the cozy bar serving up delicious cocktails and hear the sizzle of meat from the table grills . . . and most definitely hear that Pat Benatar song in the karaoke rooms.

Insa has been in the making for about two years now, as I write this, and we are finally at the stage of picking out paint for the bathroom walls and setting up our walk-in with Michael Stokes (chef de cuisine) and Yong Shin (our sous-chef and partner). Soon our friend Rigo Vazquez from The Good Fork will join us in making vats and vats of kimchee and Jamie Seet will be training the servers on how to grill meat Korean style. I feel the butterflies again in my stomach as we plan for our opening in a few months, just as I had a week before Ben and I opened the doors of The Good Fork.

Our formula is still the same—great food, aesthetic, and service—but this time around, we go into the experiment knowing a lot more than we knew ten years ago. It's much more collaborative; it's not just Ben and me. We have a real management team, and I'll be working with other chefs and cooks who brings other experiences and history to the menu. It's no mom-and-pop shop we are building this time around, but as Ben would say, it will be "an ultimate Korean fun-time place for celebration!" It's also the next big lesson in our lives as a cook and carpenter, but we have built a "family" of amazing people to experience it with us.

By the same token, with this book we want to share not just our recipes from the past decade and then some, but the spirit with which we live through food. Our home and The Good Fork are less than a block apart, and we are always back and forth, blurring the lines between life and work. Our new restaurant is just a ten-minute trip away, and it's around the corner from where our two kids go to school. The recipes in this book reflect that bridge between the professional kitchen and our home stove. They are what we serve our customers, feed our children, and bring to a barbecue.

We hope these recipes make their way into your life, too, either onto your table or into your daydreams of food.

SOHUI KIM, 2016

SPECIAL INGREDIENTS:

A Note About Using This Book

As a Korean cook, my pantry is always stocked with a handful of Korean ingredients that I rely on to build flavor. These are the few that you'll come across often in this book. They are widely available at almost any Asian market, can be ordered online, and these days are also sometimes found at large supermarkets or specialty food shops. Note that while substitutions will always change the flavors of a dish, I've noted below where they are possible.

DEONGJANG [dwen-jhang]: This is a salty, nutty, umami-packed Korean fermented soybean paste. It is similar to Japanese miso paste, but its flavor is more rustic and it has a slightly different funk to it, because it is made in a slightly different way. *Deongjang* is made by slowly simmering dried soybeans, which are then ground into a paste and formed into blocks called *meju*, which are hung up to dry and to ferment. (My country relatives had blocks of it hanging up on the ceiling in Korea—holy moly is it stinky!) Meju is then covered with brine in a stone vessel so it breaks down even further. The liquid is *gan-jang*, or Korean soy sauce, and the paste is the deongjang. Miso, on the other hand, is fermented with a culture called *koji*, which is rice that has been inoculated with a specific bacteria. The flavor also depends on how long it is aged: Darker, older versions of deongjang are good for soup, while lighter versions are better for the Korean Crudités Platter with Ssam Jang on page 34. If you can't find deongjang, just use regular dark miso paste, chunky if you can find it.

GAN-JANG [ghan-jang]: Traditional Korean soy sauce, as I described, is a by-product of making fermented soybean paste. You don't have to use Korean soy sauce for the recipes in this book, but be sure to buy one that is "naturally brewed" rather than created in a lab and filled with caramel coloring or preservatives. With real brewed soy sauce, you taste the complexity of the soy, not just salt. On the shelves of Asian markets these days now, there are hundreds of soy sauces from every country for everything—soups and marinades and so on. The key is to find one made from natural ingredients that tastes rich and complex, not just salty and sweet.

GOCHUJANG [go-chu-jang]: This is Korean red chile paste, which is made by fermenting a paste made of a mix of dried, seeded red Korean chile powder; sugar; glutinous rice; fermented soybeans; and salt. It is traditionally fermented in earthenware pots for years. This you will need to order online if you can't find it locally, as there's really nothing you can use as a substitute. I use it in my Korean Crudités Platter with Ssam Jang on page 34, as well as in the marinade for Kimchee Rice with Steak and Eggs on page 94.

GOCHUJARU [go-chu-karoo]: This is Korean dried red pepper flakes, made from the red, ripened form of Korean chile peppers. In this case, they are fully ripened on the plant, then sun dried. The seeds are then removed and the pods are ground into coarse or fine pepper. (*Gochu* means "chile pepper," and *jaru* means "powder.") I use coarse flakes for kimchee and finer for things like *banchan*. It also comes in all different levels of heat, so you might want to check the intensity of yours before you use it. You can use Aleppo pepper as a substitute, which has a similar hot and floral flavor, or crushed red peppers without seeds. But don't do that for kimchee; it just won't be the same.

KIMCHEE: Many of my recipes call for kimchee, which can vary widely in quality. The recipes in this book will taste best when you make your own following my directions on page 193. If you use your own or a store-bought version, you might need to adjust for seasoning.

CHEONG-GOCHU [chong-go-chu]: The fresh green version of gochujaru, also called "long hots" or "long greens." It means green peppers. You could use a mix of jalapeño or serrano chiles or even Japanese shishito peppers!

KOSHER SALT: I always use Diamond Crystal kosher salt, which has a flakier texture that is easily crumbled between your fingertips and allows you more control as you sprinkle it into a dish. It is made using a slightly different process than other kosher salts like Morton's and most standard fine sea salts and table salts. A general, but not exact, rule of thumb to follow is that 1 teaspoon fine sea or table salt = 1¼ teaspoons Morton's kosher salt = 1¾ teaspoons Diamond Crystal kosher salt. In other words, you would use less of most kinds of salt than Diamond Crystal. Be sure to adjust your measurements accordingly if you want to make a substitution.

MYEOL CHI AEK JEOT [myul-chee-eck-jeot]: This is the Korean answer to the fermented fish sauce found in Thailand and Vietnam, except ours is mostly made with anchovies rather than shrimp or other fish. Most people just refer to it as *aek jeot*, or fish sauce. Korea is a peninsula, so anchovies are everywhere. In English, you'll see it listed as "anchovy sauce," often next to soy sauce in stores. In this book, I usually just call for regular fish sauce, but if you can find the Korean version, by all means use it.

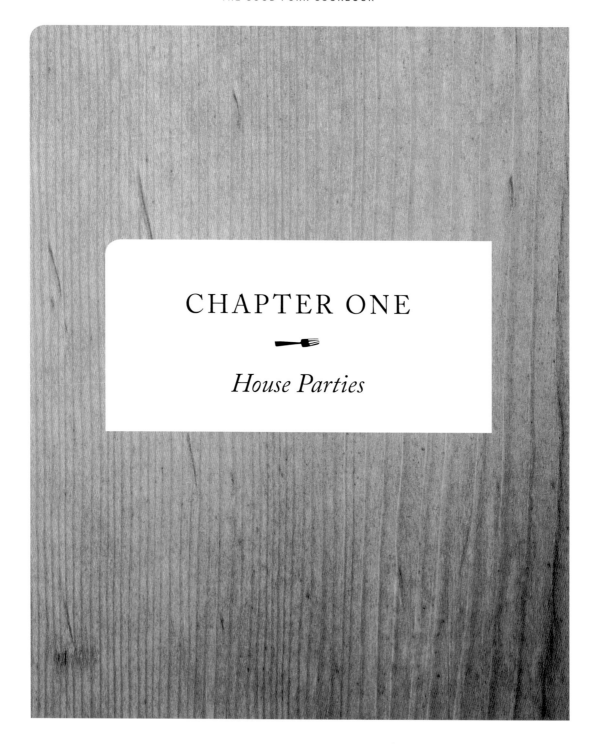

CHAPTER ONE

House Parties

BEN AND I REALLY MOVED TO RED HOOK BECAUSE OF A HOUSE. Ben had a friend in the neighborhood, and he had already fallen for its mix of pretty, old row houses, waterfront industrial zones, and grit—hard to find in New York City these days. And then he found this old row house: It was the right time and it was still "cheap" to buy here then. I remember looking at it—"Honey, you gotta see the backyard," Ben said—and I was thinking, "You can't buy this house. Briscoe and Green find dead bodies floating two blocks away on *Law & Order* all the time! (*Clang Clang*)."

Plus, it was a dump. When Ben bought it with his sister Julia (he and I weren't yet married, and we all lived there together for a few years), it was filled with junk. It took four Dumpsters just to clean out the debris because the people who lived there prior were hoarders.

That is the only time so far I've been wrong about a big decision in our relationship. With incredible dedication and focus, Ben has turned a dilapidated old house into a great place for celebration and conviviality, and the backyard into an outdoor Shangri-la. The latter has a huge, century-old oak in an unusually wide and ample backyard, where Ben built a wet bar and a makeshift outdoor kitchen for me. It became a special place, one we wanted to share with family and friends. We got married in that backyard, and so did several of our friends. We have hosted eight weddings, where we would have 150 to 180 people, sometimes three whole pigs, and a crawfish boil. For my own wedding, I was fortunate to have a sushi chef I knew from my days at the Sony Club who made sushi while guests sipped on prosecco, soju, and sake. And Ben has put on plays back there—real productions with sets and tickets. We call it the Coffey St. Playhouse, after the name of our street.

When Ben bought the house, I happened to have cooking jobs that were somehow not all about late nights and weekends. We were able to put on all kinds of parties—some planned, some just "Hey, come over and bring a six-pack!" It was a period of my life as a chef or, really, as a cook when I developed a sense of catering in the truest sense. By which I mean giving to the people I know and love, and also experimenting with what I really like to cook myself. So these are the recipes in this chapter: Things I made for our own parties, and for my family and my friends.

BEET SALAD

WITH *oranges, grilled scallions,* AND *black sesame paste*

SERVES 4 TO 6

I have to confess that when I set out to update this recipe for this book, I realized the original had the title of "Beet Salad, Goat Cheese, Romaine, Candied Walnuts, and Pickled Apple." I joked that 2002 called and they want their beet salad with goat cheese back. It's true, I proudly served that salad ten years ago at parties—everybody did!—and even made little goat cheese fritters. Those still taste very wonderful together, but it doesn't seem as fresh to me as it did back then. That's why I am giving you this recipe instead, a dish recently updated by our chef de cuisine Sam Filloramo, one of my favorite cooks of all time (you can read more about him in chapter 4). The sesame, grilled scallions, and oranges bring bling to the beets and make them sing in a brand-new way, while totally keeping with the original style and flavor profiles of The Good Fork. If you can't find yuzu juice (yuzu is a great sour Japanese citrus fruit, most often sold here as bottled juice), fresh lime juice is fine.

> **TIP** *To really make this salad shine, call on your inner Pollock or Krasner to haphazardly brush the black sesame seed paste onto a large platter before you layer on the beets and oranges.*

FOR THE **SALAD**

4	medium beets, scrubbed and cleaned
2	tablespoons extra-virgin olive oil
	Kosher salt
1	bunch scallions, roots trimmed
1	orange, peel and pith removed, cut crosswise into 1/4-inch (6-mm)-thick slices

FOR THE **SESAME SEED PASTE**

1/2	cup (60 g) black sesame seeds, plus extra for garnish
1/4	cup (60 ml) sesame oil
1	tablespoon honey
1/4	teaspoon kosher salt

FOR THE **BEET VINAIGRETTE**

1/2	roasted beet (see directions)
2	tablespoons soy sauce
4	teaspoons whole-grain mustard
1/2	small shallot, roughly chopped
4	teaspoons yuzu or fresh lime juice
1 1/2	teaspoons honey
1/2	cup (120 ml) grapeseed oil

RECIPE FOLLOWS

Preheat the oven to 450°F (230°C).

Make the salad: Place the beets in a medium ovenproof skillet—do not trim or peel them—and rub them with 1 tablespoon of the olive oil and a few generous pinches of salt. Add 1 cup (240 ml) water to the pan and cover it tightly with foil. Roast the beets for 1 hour, or until they are easily pierced with the tines of a fork. Remove the beets from the skillet to cool.

Wipe the skillet clean; add the scallions to the skillet, then add the remaining 1 tablespoon of olive oil and a pinch of salt. Toss to mix and roast uncovered for 15 minutes, or until soft and slightly browned, then set aside.

When the beets are cool enough to touch, trim off the tops and peel them by rubbing the skin off with a clean dishtowel or paper towel. Set aside half a beet for the vinaigrette; cut the remaining beets into ½-inch (12-mm) wedges and set them aside. Cut the scallions into 2-inch (5-cm) pieces and set them aside.

Make the sesame seed paste: Toast the sesame seeds in a small skillet over medium heat, stirring constantly until they smell toasty, about 1 minute. In a blender, grind the toasted sesame seeds, then add ½ cup (120 ml) water, a little at a time, blending until a paste forms. With the blender running, slowly drizzle in the sesame oil to make an emulsion. (It's important to add both the water and oil slowly, so the mixture does not break.) Add the honey and salt, and blend just to combine. Refrigerate the mixture until you prepare the salad.

Make the vinaigrette: In a blender or small food processor, combine the reserved ½ beet, soy sauce, mustard, shallot, yuzu juice, and honey and puree until the mixture is relatively smooth. With the blender or food processor running, drizzle in the grapeseed oil slowly until an emulsion forms. Set aside while you make the salad. (This will make about 1 cup/240 ml; any extra dressing should be refrigerated and used within a week.)

Finish the salad: Toss the beets in 3 tablespoons of the dressing. Brush the black sesame seed paste onto a large platter, then layer on the oranges and beets. Top with the scallion pieces and garnish with a teaspoon of sesame seeds. Drizzle the salad with additional vinaigrette as desired and serve immediately.

GRILLED ASPARAGUS

WITH *sauce gribiche*

SERVES 4

I made a version of this for my close friend's wedding in our backyard. It was spring and asparagus was in season. I was looking for an interesting sauce to serve it with and came across the French sauce gribiche—it's like vinaigrette that's dressed up with chopped soft-boiled egg, anchovies, lemon, capers, and cornichons, with flavors a little like a Caesar salad. I hadn't made it since culinary school and I was like, "What the heck, let's do it." I was so glad I did, as it has such an umami punch and an element of surprise. This is nice to make for guests when you want to impress them. The sauce is decadent but with an appealing brightness. It's best in spring, when the asparagus is very sweet and has a satisfying earthy quality. Grilling it adds smokiness and also brings out its sweetness, while watercress adds sharpness and freshness—though feel free to substitute any bright, peppery greens such as arugula, radish tops, or mustard greens.

TIP *The reduced balsamic vinegar in this recipe is a restaurant trick that turns ordinary balsamic into something closer to the extremely expensive aged version. Just simmer 1 bottle of ordinary balsamic vinegar slowly over medium heat until it has reduced by half. Better still, once you make it, it keeps indefinitely in your pantry.*

FOR THE **SAUCE GRIBICHE**

2   large eggs
1   teaspoon Dijon mustard
½   teaspoon sherry wine vinegar
¼   cup (60 ml) neutral oil, such as grapeseed or safflower
3   tablespoons minced shallot
2   tablespoons chopped fresh parsley, or a mix of fresh herbs
½   anchovy fillet, rinsed and minced
1   teaspoon capers
2   cornichons or gherkins, minced
1   teaspoon fresh lemon juice, plus extra if needed
     Kosher salt and freshly ground black pepper

FOR THE **SALAD**

2   pounds (910 g) asparagus
2   tablespoons olive oil
     Kosher salt and freshly ground black pepper
1   small bunch watercress
2   tablespoons reduced balsamic vinegar (see Tip)
     Fresh herbs, for garnish

RECIPE FOLLOWS

Make the gribiche: In a pot, cover the eggs with cold water and bring the water to a boil. Turn off the heat and cover the pot. Let stand, undisturbed, for 7 minutes; prepare a bowl of cold water. Dunk the eggs in the cold water to cool them down, and then peel them.

Cut the peeled eggs in half lengthwise and separate the yolks from the whites. Finely chop the whites, setting them aside. Place the yolks in a medium bowl with the mustard and sherry vinegar. Use a fork or whisk to mash them into a paste. Slowly drizzle in the neutral oil, blending it into the yolk mixture gradually to form an emulsion. When all the oil has been added, mix in the shallot, parsley, anchovy, capers, cornichons, and lemon juice. Taste and season with salt, pepper, and more lemon juice if desired. Set aside while you make the rest of the salad.

Make the salad: Heat a gas or charcoal grill or a stovetop grill pan to high, or preheat the oven to 450°F (230°C).

In a large mixing bowl, toss the asparagus with the olive oil and season it liberally with salt and pepper. Grill it or roast it on a baking sheet in the oven until it is tender and browned at the edges, 7 to 10 minutes on the grill or 10 to 15 minutes in the oven.

Meanwhile, arrange the watercress on a platter. Lay the grilled asparagus over the top. Spoon the gribiche onto the asparagus and drizzle it with the reduced balsamic. Serve it immediately, garnished with additional herbs.

MANCHEGO CHEESE FRITTERS

WITH *tomato jam*

MAKES 45 FRITTERS; SERVES 12 TO 15

Like the bread puddings on pages 107 and 171, this is one of many ways I like to use up leftover bread. You might think they would be heavy, but in fact they are lighter than most fritters. The bread disappears into these fluffy orbs that are deeply flavored with two intense salty cheeses. They are fantastic, but in all honesty what really makes this dish is the tomato jam, which your friends will want to eat with a spoon. It is great on anything—such as biscuits or served with bread and cheese.

FOR THE **FRITTERS**

1	cup (240 ml) heavy cream
3	large eggs, beaten
½	cup (120 ml) milk
8	cups (280 g) 1-inch (2.5-cm) cubes ciabatta or French bread
1½	cups (165 g) grated Manchego cheese
½	cup (55 g) grated Parmigiano-Reggiano cheese
¼	cup (13 g) chopped fresh parsley leaves
1	tablespoon chopped fresh chives
½	teaspoon fresh thyme leaves, or ⅛ teaspoon dried thyme
2	cups (160 g) panko
	Canola or safflower oil, for frying
	Freshly ground black pepper
	Chopped mint leaves, for garnish

FOR THE **TOMATO JAM**

2	tablespoons extra-virgin olive oil
1	can (28 ounces/794 g) whole canned plum tomatoes, drained
¼	cup (55 g) tightly packed light brown sugar
3	tablespoons red wine vinegar
1	tablespoon tomato paste
1	teaspoon fresh thyme leaves, or ¼ teaspoon dried thyme
	Kosher salt and freshly ground black pepper

Make the batter the day before you plan to serve the fritters. In a large mixing bowl, whisk together the cream, eggs, and milk. Add the bread cubes, both cheeses, and the herbs and stir to mix thoroughly. Cover and refrigerate overnight.

Make the tomato jam: In a skillet over medium heat, warm the olive oil. Add the tomatoes and cook, stirring occasionally, until they fall apart and are slightly caramelized, about 12 minutes. Add the brown sugar, vinegar, tomato paste, and thyme. Continue to cook, stirring frequently, until the mixture is glossy and jam-like, about 5 minutes. Season with salt and pepper. Set aside, or cover and refrigerate for up to 2 weeks.

Make the fritters: Shape the dough into 1½-inch (4-cm) balls, roll them in the panko, and set them on a plate or baking sheet.

Heat 2 inches (5 cm) of frying oil in a deep, heavy-bottomed pot to 365°F (185°C) or until a breadcrumb sizzles when you drop it in. Place a wire rack on another baking sheet.

Fry the fritters in batches, monitoring the temperature of the oil and making sure not to crowd the pan. Cook each batch until it is dark golden brown and crispy, 2 to 3 minutes, then remove with a slotted spoon to the wire rack.

Sprinkle pepper and chopped mint over the fritters and serve them while they are still hot, accompanied by warmed or room temperature tomato jam.

KOREAN CRUDITÉS PLATTER

WITH *ssam jang*

SERVES 10 TO 15

Where most people might put out an ordinary blue cheese dip when friends come over, this dip is my party go-to. The umami-packed *ssam jang*—whose base is a mix of *deongjang*, the chunky, nutty version of Korean miso paste, and the fermented red pepper spice paste called *gochujang*—can be served with a beautiful mix of crunchy and colorful vegetables and, ideally, Manchego Cheese Fritters (recipe on page 33). I admit that this pairing is not really a new idea: It's traditional to eat ssam jang with raw vegetables in Korea; it's just presented here in an American-by-way-of-France crudités platter. I remember as a child in Korea, we'd always have a snack of fresh quartered cucumbers with ssam jang (followed by tomatoes with sugar and salt for dessert!) and at Korean barbecue restaurants, ssam jang is what we dollop on the crisp lettuce leaves before we wrap them with herbs around grilled meats. Note that you should adjust the amount of gochujang you add to yours depending on how spicy you want your ssam jang to be.

> **TIP** *These are my favorite picks for the vegetables, but you could really use any mix that you like or that you have on hand. Just blanch anything in the cabbage family—bok choy, cauliflower, broccoli. When blanching, be sure to add salt to both the water you bring to a boil and the water you prepare for chilling—it vastly improves the flavor and color of blanched vegetables.*

FOR THE SSAM JANG

- ¾ cup (180 ml) deongjang (Korean fermented soybean paste; see page 20)
- ¼ to 1 cup (60 to 240 ml) gochujang (Korean red chile paste; see page 21)
- 2 cloves garlic, minced
- 2 tablespoons honey
- 2 tablespoons sesame oil
- 1 tablespoon grated fresh peeled ginger
- 1 tablespoon toasted sesame seeds

FOR THE VEGETABLES

- 1 bunch red breakfast radishes, preferably with their greens
- 1 red bell pepper, cut into strips
- 1 orange or yellow bell pepper, cut into strips
- 1 large fennel bulb with the fronds, cut lengthwise into long, skinny wedges

  Florets from 1 large head broccoli, blanched and cooled
- 2 Persian cucumbers, quartered lengthwise into long spears

Make the ssam jang: In a medium bowl, combine the deongjang, ¼ cup (60 ml) of the gochujang, the garlic, honey, sesame oil, ginger, and sesame seeds and whisk well. Taste and add more gochujang to your preference for spiciness.

Refrigerate the ssam jang if you are not serving the crudités in the next hour or two. It will keep in a covered jar in the refrigerator for at least a month. Just bring it to room temperature before serving.

Serve the vegetables scattered around a large platter, mixing them around the plate for visual appeal, with the ssam jang in a small, decorative bowl in the center.

KIMCHEE STRUDEL

SERVES 8 TO 10

Kimchee is the new bacon—meaning it just makes everything taste better. This is my twist on a Greek spanakopita, but made with kimchee. The idea came to me one day when I had a lot of leftover phyllo dough. For our parties years ago, I would always make little rolled savory pastries—Moroccans would call them *cigares*—filled with mushrooms and ginger. I've found that you can put almost anything in phyllo, and it tastes great . . . so why not do a version flavored with the condiment I love the most? The result is better than the original, and still seems exciting today.

2	cups (70 g) dried shiitake mushrooms
2	cups (560 g) chopped kimchee (page 193)
2	tablespoons canola oil
1	medium onion, sliced 1/4 inch (6 mm) thick
5	cloves garlic, minced
1	(3-inch/7.5-cm) piece fresh ginger, peeled and grated
1	tablespoon sugar
1	tablespoon sake
1	tablespoon soy sauce
1	tablespoon sesame oil
10	sheets phyllo dough, fresh or thawed
1/2	cup (1 stick/115 g) unsalted butter, melted Mae ploy (Thai sweet chile sauce) for dipping (optional)

In a small bowl, soak the mushrooms in very hot but not boiling water for 15 minutes. Drain them (you can save the liquid for stock), remove any long stems, and slice them very thinly. Set them aside.

Place the kimchee in a strainer in the sink, and use a fork to press out most of the juice. Set aside.

In a large skillet, heat the canola oil over medium heat. Add the onion and cook, stirring, until it is soft but does not brown. Stir in the garlic and continue to cook for another minute. Stir in the ginger and cook for another minute. Add the soaked mushrooms and cook, stirring occasionally, for 5 minutes more. Add the strained kimchee and cook for three more minutes. Stir in the sugar, sake, soy sauce, and sesame oil, then turn off the heat and allow the mixture to cool until it is just warm or at room temperature.

You will need 5 sheets of phyllo dough for each strudel. Lay 1 sheet on a large cutting board. Brush the entire sheet with melted butter using a pastry brush. Lay another sheet on top of it and repeat until you have brushed all 5 sheets with butter.

Put half the filling in the middle of the buttered stack of phyllo dough. Shape the filling into a long, narrow rectangle, with at least 4 inches (10 cm) of space at each end of the rectangle. Fold in those ends, then fold over the sides, so that you've wrapped up the filling like a burrito. Brush a little butter into the seam where the sides meet, then brush the entire outside of the strudel with butter. Place the strudel on a parchment-lined or greased baking sheet. Repeat with the remaining phyllo and filling. (You can make the strudels up to this point and then freeze them until you are ready to bake, without defrosting them.)

To bake the strudels, preheat the oven to 325°F (165°C). Bake until golden brown, about 20 minutes. Cut them into 2-inch (5-cm) servings with a serrated knife just before you serve them. Serve them warm or at room temperature—but within a few hours of baking them—with sweet chile sauce for dipping, if you like.

CRAB CAKES

WITH *sriracha aioli*

MAKES ABOUT 1 DOZEN CRAB CAKES; SERVES 6

Though I often made at these home, I hadn't ever intended to serve them at the restaurant. But Ben said the menu needed another crowd-pleaser like the dumplings. I told him, "Hey, it's not TGI Friday's we're running here. I want our menu to be special." It was a real fight, and one that he won. He reminded me that I made the best crab cakes he'd ever tasted. He's my biggest fan, but I agree, they are good. The key to crab cakes is the technique: The first rule is, don't use too much filler. I am always disappointed when I order crab cakes somewhere and they are either too bready or I can't taste the crab at all. Good seafood these days is very expensive, so this dish is a special-occasion splurge. When you see great crabmeat, treat yourself!

TIP *Fresh crab is best, but pasteurized is a fine alternative if it isn't produced on giant farms in Indonesia, Thailand, Vietnam, or China. Do as I do, and check www.seafoodwatch.org for a rundown on which fish to buy and which to avoid.*

1	pound (455 g) fresh crabmeat, drained and cleaned of any pieces of shell (see Tip)
2	tablespoons butter
½	large onion, finely diced
2	small shallots, finely diced
1	large leek, white and light green parts minced
	Kosher salt and freshly ground black pepper
1½	cups (120 g) panko, plus extra for coating
¾	cup (180 ml) mayonnaise
¼	cup (13 g) fresh parsley leaves, minced
1	lemon, zested and juiced
4	to 5 tablespoons (60 to 75 ml) vegetable oil
	Sriracha Aioli (recipe follows)

Drain the crabmeat in a colander.

In a skillet, melt the butter over medium heat and cook the onion, shallots, and leek until lightly caramelized, 8 to 10 minutes. Season with salt and pepper and let cool in a large bowl.

Add the crabmeat, panko, mayonnaise, parsley, lemon zest, and half of the lemon juice. Mix by hand, making sure not to break up the crab pieces. A small ball should hold together loosely when pressed gently between your hands; if not, adjust the consistency with more panko or mayonnaise. Taste the mixture and adjust the seasoning with more salt, pepper, and lemon juice as needed.

Use a 2-inch (5-cm) ring mold or biscuit cutter to form the crab cakes. Fill the mold with 1½ inches (4 cm) of crab mixture, coat the top and bottom of the cake with more panko, and then remove the cake to a plate or baking sheet.

When all the crab cakes are formed, heat the oil in a large skillet over medium-high heat. Once the oil begins to shimmer, add the crab cakes—working in batches if you need to—and panfry them until they're golden brown on both sides and heated through.

Serve immediately with sriracha aioli and a simple salad, if you like.

SRIRACHA AIOLI

MAKES ⅔ CUP (165 ML)

Aioli is a fancy way of saying "mayo," but it is very easy to make. Once you start making it at home, you'll never buy the jarred stuff again. (Unless you like the flavor of Hellman's, which I must admit, I actually do sometimes!) Sriracha hot sauce seems so ubiquitous now, and rightly so—it packs a uniquely yummy punch and sweet heat. This aioli can be used for a myriad of things: sandwiches, little toasts layered with fat mussels, these crab cakes, and as an accompaniment to anything fried!

TIP *My culinary school trick for whisking together the aioli is to coil a clean, damp dish rag into a doughnut shape, and then place the mixing bowl on top of it. The towel keeps the bowl steady and in place. If at any point your mixture breaks down and separates instead of getting thick and creamy, don't despair. Just put a fresh egg yolk in a new bowl, and slowly whisk the broken mixture into it, just as you would the oil, then continue adding the oil as per the recipe.*

½ teaspoon kosher salt, plus more if needed
1 small clove garlic
1 egg yolk
½ cup (120 ml) canola or grapeseed oil
1 tablespoon fresh lemon juice
1 to 3 teaspoons sriracha hot sauce

Using a mortar and pestle or by scraping the back of your knife on a cutting board, make a paste of the salt and garlic. Scrape the paste into a large bowl. Whisk in ½ teaspoon water, then the egg yolk.

Very gradually drip the oil down the side of the bowl into the yolk mixture while constantly stirring with a whisk. The mixture should emulsify and thicken. When it starts to get very thick, mix in the lemon juice, then continue to drizzle in the rest of the oil.

When all the oil has been incorporated, mix in the hot sauce. Adjust the salt to taste, or add a little more water if the aioli seems too thick. Cover and refrigerate for up to 1 week.

KOREAN BOUILLABAISSE

SERVES 6

I love bouillabaisse or cioppino—in fact almost every country with abundant seafood has some kind of fish stew. Korea, too. The real Korean version, called *meuntang*, is spicier and has cod or pollock and chiles. This is a milder version that appeals to a larger audience. I first made this for a wedding. I thought it would be fun to make a fish stock; I used a fish head—a big old head of cod—and played around with some Korean ingredients, like kimchee. Eventually, it worked its way onto The Good Fork menu as a special whenever we had some really good fish or fish heads. It's just spot-on in the summer. When I can find it, I use Korean parsley to top this soup. It's a slightly heartier version of parsley that is used more like a vegetable than an herb but tastes fairly similar to Italian flat-leaf parsley. Here you want the greens to function not as a condiment but as a part of the dish, so if you can't find Korean parsley, use watercress instead of regular parsley.

2	tablespoons canola oil
1	cup (130 g) thinly sliced onion
4	cloves garlic, minced
2	cups (560 g) chopped kimchee (page 193)
3	cups (420 g) 3/4-inch (2-cm) cubes potato
1	tablespoon gochujaru (Korean dried red pepper flakes, page 21), or any crushed red chile flakes
2	teaspoons soy sauce
2	teaspoons fish sauce
1	quart (960 ml) Japanese Dashi (recipe follows)
2	cups (480 ml) chicken stock
1 1/2	pounds (680 g) cod steaks, cut into 2-inch (5-cm) chunks, or use any flaky white fish
1	pound (455 g) clams or mussels, scrubbed and debearded
12	large shrimp (about 3/4 pound/340 g), peeled and deveined
	Kosher salt and freshly ground black pepper
4	scallions, thinly sliced
1	cup (25 g) Korean parsley or watercress, tough stems removed

In a large pot, heat the oil over medium heat and sauté the onion for 1 minute. Add the garlic and cook, stirring occasionally, until the onion and garlic are soft and translucent, about 5 minutes. Add the chopped kimchee and sauté until it darkens and caramelizes slightly but doesn't brown, about 5 minutes more.

Add the potato, gochujaru, soy sauce, and fish sauce. Add the dashi and chicken stock, bring to a low boil, and simmer for about 12 minutes, until the potatoes are just cooked.

Add the fish, clams, and shrimp. Cover the pot and simmer until the clams open up, about 5 minutes. Taste for seasoning and adjust with salt and pepper (or more chopped kimchee). Divide the soup among six bowls and top each bowl with scallions and Korean parsley. Serve immediately.

JAPANESE DASHI

MAKES 1 QUART (960 ML)

This is a lighter version than Korean Dashi (page 205), which is made with dried anchovies. I usually save the kombu from this recipe for the Soybean Sprout Salad banchan (page 188) or toss it with a little soy sauce to put in the Miso Ramen on page 183.

1 ounce (28 g) dried kombu seaweed
1 packed cup (½ ounce/14 g) bonito flakes

In a large pot, bring the kombu and 5 cups (1.2 L) water to a simmer but not a full boil. Add the bonito flakes and turn off the heat. Let them steep for at least 15 minutes and up to 2 hours.

Strain and discard the bonito flakes and kombu. Cover and refrigerate the dashi for up to to 1 week.

VIETNAMESE-STYLE ST. LOUIS RIBS

WITH *pickled summer vegetable salad* AND *Chinese sausage and scallion corn bread*

SERVES 6 TO 8

I originally made these ribs for the wedding of my friends Billy and Jenny, one of many sets of couples who got married in our backyard. But I've always made this marinade—I use it on chicken, too—which is inspired by the flavors you often find in Vietnamese cooking. Mix brown sugar, fish sauce, kaffir lime leaves, and lemongrass: Presto, it tastes like Vietnam. For the wedding, I riffed on the Southern barbecue meat-and-three theme and served the ribs with an Asian coleslaw and corn bread, a combination I eventually upgraded over the years to the pickled summer vegetable salad and Chinese sausage and scallion corn bread recipes I've included here.

FOR THE MARINADE AND RIBS

1 ½ cups (360 ml) fish sauce

½ cup (110 g) packed light brown sugar

¼ cup (40 g) minced garlic

¼ cup (50 g) minced peeled fresh ginger

1 stalk lemongrass, white parts chopped and light green parts bruised with the back of a knife

4 kaffir lime leaves, chopped

2 or 3 bird's eye chiles, bruised with the back of a knife

2 racks St. Louis ribs (about 5 pounds/2.25 kg)

FOR THE APRICOT GLAZE

⅓ cup (75 ml) apricot jam

¼ cup (60 ml) rice wine vinegar

¼ teaspoon freshly ground black pepper

Pickled Summer Vegetable Salad (recipe follows)

Chinese Sausage and Scallion Corn Bread (recipe follows)

At least 24 and up to 48 hours before you plan to serve the ribs, make the marinade: In a large bowl, combine 3 cups (720 ml) water, the fish sauce, brown sugar, garlic, ginger, lemongrass, lime leaves, and chiles. Stir to mix well.

Place the ribs in a large Pyrex or ceramic baking dish just big enough to fit the racks. Pour the marinade over the ribs so that it covers them completely. Cover and refrigerate them to marinate for 24 to 48 hours.

Make the ribs: Preheat the oven to 275°F (135°C). Pour off the marinade from the ribs, reserving 1 cup (240 ml) of the marinade. Pour the reserved marinade and 1 cup (240 ml) water over the ribs in the baking dish. Roast them for 2 to 2½ hours, until the meat is a bit wobbly but not falling off the bone. Tear off a small piece to taste: If it's sinewy, return the pan to the oven.

When the ribs are tender, remove them from the oven and let them cool to room temperature. Discard the marinade and refrigerate the ribs until you are ready to grill them—they will keep in the refrigerator up to 2 days—or finish them right away.

To grill the ribs, heat a gas or charcoal grill or a stovetop grill pan to medium-high.

Make the glaze: In a bowl, whisk together the jam, vinegar, and pepper to make a glaze that is thick enough to stick to the ribs but thin enough to paint on with a basting brush.

Using a sharp knife, separate the racks into individual ribs. Grill for a few minutes on each side, until well-marked and heated through.

Remove the ribs from the grill, brush them generously with the glaze, and continue to grill them until the glaze caramelizes. Remove them to a clean platter and serve with the pickled summer vegetable salad and Chinese sausage and scallion corn bread.

PICKLED SUMMER VEGETABLE SALAD

SERVES 6 TO 8

I originally made this as a slaw. I was looking for crunch and brightness, something acidic to serve with the rich ribs to satisfy the whole notion of "cutting the fat." (Even though you still eat the fat, so there's no cutting anything!) Over the years, I've turned that simple slaw into a more interesting salad of quick-pickled vegetables that's a little more intensely flavored and textured. Note that you can also use radishes or jicama instead of carrots or kohlrabi, and if you have a mandoline, by all means use it.

½   cup (120 ml) rice wine vinegar

3   tablespoons sugar

1   tablespoon kosher salt

3   medium carrots, peeled and cut into 2 by ¼-inch (5-cm by 6-mm) matchstick strips

1   small bulb kohlrabi, peeled and cut into 2 by ¼-inch (5-cm by 6-mm) matchstick strips

2   Persian cucumbers or ½ English cucumber, cut on a diagonal into ¼-inch (6-mm)-thick slices

½   small red cabbage, thinly sliced (about 2 cups/190 g)

⅓   cup (17 g) fresh Thai basil leaves

⅓   cup (17 g) fresh mint leaves

Make the brine by combining ½ cup (120 ml) water, the vinegar, sugar, and salt in a small saucepan over medium-high heat. Heat the liquid until it almost reaches a simmer.

In a large heatproof bowl, combine the carrots and kohlrabi. Pour the hot brine over them and let stand for 5 minutes.

Drain the carrots and kohlrabi and return them to the bowl. Add the cucumbers and cabbage, tossing to mix.

Refrigerate until chilled. When ready to serve, tear the basil and mint into smaller pieces by hand and add them to the vegetables, tossing to mix. Serve the salad cold or at room temperature.

CHINESE SAUSAGE AND SCALLION CORN BREAD

SERVES 6 TO 8

When I worked in other restaurant kitchens before opening The Good Fork, I always made corn bread when it was my turn to make staff meals. Each line cook is given a day when they have to cook for their colleagues, and you're told what to use, often something inexpensive or that isn't going to get used for service. Easy, cheap, and fast, corn bread is a perfect vehicle for all kinds of flavors or additions. This version came about because I used to make pigs in a blanket for parties with cured Chinese sausage, which has a sweet-savory flavor and is thin like the little smoked sausages you would usually use. I had some left over that was already cut up, so I just added it to a corn bread batter with some scallions. It was so good, I've been making it ever since. You can follow my lead and substitute any other herbs or cooked or cured sausages that you like.

4	tablespoons (½ stick/115 g) unsalted butter
5	Chinese sausages (about 190 g), cut into ¼-inch (6-mm) slices, then diced
1 ½	cups (190 g) all-purpose flour
1 ½	cups (270 g) fine cornmeal
¼	cup (50 g) sugar
1 ½	teaspoons baking powder
1	teaspoon kosher salt
¼	teaspoon freshly ground black pepper
2	cups (480 ml) buttermilk, at room temperature
2	large eggs, beaten
1	bunch scallions, thinly sliced

Preheat the oven to 350°F (175°C). In an 8-inch (20-cm) cast-iron skillet over low heat, melt the butter. Pour out the melted butter, setting it aside for later use. Return the skillet to the stove.

Raise the heat to medium and cook the diced sausage in the skillet, stirring occasionally, until it crisps around the edges, about 3 minutes. With a slotted spoon, remove the sausage to a bowl or plate and set it aside. Remove the pan from the heat, swirl the sausage fat around the pan to generously coat the bottom and sides, then pour off any excess fat and discard. Set the pan aside while you make the batter.

In a large bowl, whisk together the flour, cornmeal, sugar, baking powder, salt, and pepper. In another bowl, whisk together the buttermilk and eggs, then whisk in the reserved melted butter.

Make a well in the dry ingredients and pour the wet ingredients into the well. Mix briefly, until most of the dry ingredients are moistened but the batter is still lumpy. Fold in the scallions and the cooked sausage, being careful not overmix—there will still be a few dry patches.

Pour the batter into the fat-covered skillet, using a spatula to spread it into an even layer. Bake for 40 minutes, or until the sides have pulled away from the pan and a toothpick or metal skewer comes out clean. Let cool in the pan for 15 minutes, invert onto a cutting board, and cut into squares or wedges.

FRESH PASTA DOUGH

MAKES ABOUT 3 POUNDS (1.4 KG) OF PASTA DOUGH

This is my master pasta dough recipe, which you can use to make all the pastas in this book, including the Butternut Squash Agnolotti with Mushroom Consommé, Lemon, and Swiss Chard (page 51). I learned to make pasta from some of the best chefs, and over time I learned the tweaks. Many recipes for fresh pasta dough call for Italian "00" flour, which is perfect for pasta but hard to find. That's why this recipe is my go-to, because it also makes great pasta with only all-purpose flour, so you can make it anywhere, anytime. If you can find semolina, however, substituting a little bit for the all-purpose flour gives your pasta a better texture.

> **TIP** *For this recipe, you will need a pasta machine or an attachment for a food processor or stand mixer to roll and cut the dough.*

2 ½   cups (315 g) all-purpose flour, plus extra for dusting

1   cup (180 g) semolina flour, or substitute all-purpose flour (125 g)

1   tablespoon kosher salt

5   large eggs

1   to 2 tablespoons extra-virgin olive oil

RECIPE CONTINUES

In a large mixing bowl, combine the flour, semolina (if using), and salt. Make a well in the center of the flour and crack the eggs into the well.

Using a fork, carefully beat together the eggs in the well. Add 1 tablespoon oil and gently mix it with the eggs.

Gradually begin mixing the flour into the eggs with the fork, drawing it in from the sides of the bowl. When the egg and flour mixture becomes too thick to stir with the fork, use your hands to slowly mix in the rest of the flour. Add up to another tablespoon of oil to help the dough come together, then if needed, up to 2 tablespoons water. For cut pasta, such as fettuccine, the dough should be firm and a little bouncy, but workable. For shaped pastas, like ravioli or agnolotti, the dough should have a more pliable consistency, and thus just a little bit more water will help.

Lightly flour your work surface and knead the dough until it is smooth and soft, like a baby's bottom—not long, about 2 minutes. Wrap the dough tightly with plastic and let it rest at room temperature for 30 minutes to 2 hours, to allow the gluten to relax so the pasta will be less brittle and more workable.

FOR FILLED PASTAS:

If you are making the agnolotti on page 51 or ravioli on page 53, you only need to use half of this recipe. (Cut the dough in half and then freeze one half for up to a month for later use, bringing it slowly to room temperature before you use it.)

Divide the remaining half into fourths. Press each fourth of dough into a rectangle thin enough to roll through the pasta machine on the thickest setting. Once it goes through, fold the flattened rectangle in thirds, and run it through the thickest setting again.

Working on progressively thinner settings, roll the dough through each setting twice until you've rolled out each piece into thin sheets about 5 inches by 3 feet (12 by 91.5 cm) long. Prepare the filled pasta immediately, following the instructions for the agnolotti on page 51 or ravioli on page 53.

To cook any shape of filled pasta, bring a large pot of salted water to a rolling boil. Cook the pasta, preferably in small batches so that it doesn't crowd the pot, until it is al dente, about 1½ minutes. Drain and serve immediately.

FOR CUT PASTAS:

To make the fettuccine on page 55, use the entire recipe and divide the dough into fourths. Press each fourth of dough into a rectangle thin enough to roll through the pasta machine on the thickest setting. Once it goes through, fold the flattened rectangle in thirds, and run it through the thickest setting again.

Working on progressively thinner settings, roll the dough through each setting twice until you've rolled out each piece into thin sheets about 5 inches by 3 feet (12 by 91.5 cm). Dust the dough with flour so it doesn't stick to itself, gently roll it up like a jelly roll, and cut it into ¼-inch (6-mm) strips.

Separate the strips, dust them with flour, and cook within a minute or two; otherwise, hang them up to dry on a rack or the back of a chair until you're ready to use them.

To cook any shape of homemade pasta, bring a large pot of salted water to a rolling boil. Cook the pasta, preferably in small batches so that it doesn't crowd the pot, until it is al dente, about 1½ minutes. Drain and serve immediately.

BUTTERNUT SQUASH AGNOLOTTI

WITH *mushroom consommé, lemon,* AND *Swiss chard*

SERVES 8

This comes from my culinary school days, when I was chosen as one of three students to represent our school at a serious competition in Chicago. We came up with our own menu: this agnolotti, whose extra folds scoop up the consommé, Shiraz-braised short ribs, and a tangerine crème caramel. I made this dish a lot beforehand to practice. We won. (It was a great team: Joncarl Lachman, Caryn Stabinsky, and Mike Ventura—this one's for you!)

TIP *You can make the consommé and roasted squash in advance, and you can also freeze the agnolotti.*

FOR THE **SQUASH**

Vegetable oil

1   large butternut squash (2 pounds/910 g)

FOR THE **CONSOMMÉ**

10   ounces (300 g) fresh cremini mushrooms

6   ounces (180 g) fresh shiitake mushrooms

10   ounces (300 g) fresh oyster mushrooms

3   sprigs fresh thyme

4   cloves garlic, peeled and crushed

1   large shallot, sliced

3   tablespoons olive oil

Kosher salt and freshly ground black pepper

FOR THE **AGNOLOTTI**

3/4   cup (185 g) fresh ricotta, drained

1/2   cup (120 ml) mascarpone cheese

1/4   cup (25 g) grated Parmigiano-Reggiano cheese

1   teaspoon minced fresh sage

Kosher salt and freshly ground black pepper

1/2   batch fresh pasta dough (page 47)

All-purpose flour for dusting

1   large egg, beaten

FOR THE **GARNISH**

4   Swiss chard leaves, cut into 2 by 1/4-inch (5-cm by 6-mm) matchstick strips

1/2   cup (50 g) shaved Parmigiano-Reggiano cheese

Zest of 1 lemon (about 1 tablespoon)

RECIPE FOLLOWS

Roast the squash: Preheat the oven to 450°F (230°C) and grease a large baking sheet with the vegetable oil. Halve the squash and scoop out the seeds, then roast it facedown on the greased pan until it is fork-tender, about 45 minutes.

While the squash cooks, line a colander with cheesecloth. When the squash is done, scoop out the flesh and drain it in the colander for at least half an hour, preferably refrigerated overnight. Refrigerate until you make the agnolotti.

Make the consommé: Preheat the oven to 425°F (220°C). Brush any dirt off the mushrooms and place them on a baking sheet, then toss them with the thyme, garlic, shallot, and olive oil, making sure they are scattered evenly on the pan and not piled up on top of each other. Season them with 2 teaspoons salt, then black pepper to taste, and roast them until browned and fragrant, about 20 minutes.

Transfer the roasted mushroom mixture to a large pot and add 2 quarts (2 L) water. Bring it to a boil, then reduce the heat to low and simmer very gently for 40 minutes. Strain the broth and discard the mushrooms and aromatics. Season the broth with salt and pepper and set it aside. This can be made up to 3 days ahead and kept refrigerated.

Make the agnolotti: Mash the cooled, drained squash into a smooth paste, then stir in the ricotta, mascarpone, grated cheese, and sage. Season liberally with salt and pepper. Put it in a pastry bag with a wide tip or a zip-top bag with a hole cut in one corner.

Follow the instructions on page 48 to roll out the pasta dough into thin sheets, about 5 inches by 3 feet (12 by 91.5 cm). Lightly flour the sheets and cut them in half. Flour your work surface, and lay out one pasta sheet horizontally.

Working about ½-inch (12 mm) from the edge closest to you, use the pastry bag to squeeze out a 1-inch (2.5-cm)-thick line of squash filling from one end of the pasta sheet to the other, leaving a ½-inch (12-mm) border at each end of the sheet.

Using a pastry brush, brush a line of egg along the dough on the edge farthest from you, parallel to the line of filling.

Working from the side closest to you, roll the dough over so that it encases the filling in a long rope. Press the edge down where you brushed the egg to seal in the filling. Roll the rope over one more time.

Using two fingers, press the dough down at 1½-inch (4-cm) intervals where you will cut it, to make little pillows. Use a fluted pastry wheel to trim it into pieces. (You can knead the trimmed bits back together and cook them immediately or freeze them. Don't refrigerate, as the dough will oxidize and take on an off flavor.)

Finish the dish: Bring a large pot of well-salted water to a boil. Cook the agnolotti in small batches, scooping them out of the boiling water and into a large bowl when they are just al dente, about 1½ minutes.

Meanwhile, reheat the consommé over medium heat until it steams and is very hot.

When all the agnolotti are cooked, divide the pasta and hot consommé among eight bowls, and top each with the Swiss chard, shaved Parmigiano-Reggiano, and lemon zest. Serve immediately.

RAVIOLI

WITH *arugula, shiitakes,* AND *ricotta in creamy brown butter*

SERVES 4 TO 6

I started making these to use up all the greens that were coming from the urban farm around the corner from us. We had a ton of arugula, and I sautéed it down and mixed it with mushrooms. It was a great combination—slightly bitter, slightly earthy. But the real trick to ravioli is making the pasta dough nice and thin. The results are so simple, but so good.

FOR THE **RAVIOLI**

3	tablespoons extra-virgin olive oil
1	medium shallot, minced
10	ounces (300 g) arugula or other mixed greens
	Kosher salt and freshly ground black pepper
1 ½	cups (200 g) thinly sliced fresh shiitake mushrooms
1	cup (245 g) ricotta cheese
	Zest of 1 lemon (about 1 tablespoon)
¼	teaspoon ground nutmeg
½	batch fresh pasta dough (page 47)
	All-purpose flour for dusting
1	large egg, beaten

FOR THE **SAUCE**

½	cup (1 stick/115 g) unsalted butter, cut into 8 uniform pieces
1	cup (240 ml) pasta cooking water
4	sprigs fresh thyme, stems removed
	Zest of 1 lemon (about 1 tablespoon)
	Freshly grated Parmigiano-Reggiano cheese, for garnish

RECIPE FOLLOWS

Make the ravioli: Prepare a colander over a bowl or in the sink. In a large skillet over medium heat, warm 2 tablespoons of the olive oil and sauté the shallot until soft and translucent, about 3 minutes.

Add the arugula and a few pinches of salt, which will help it wilt, and season it with black pepper. Cook until the greens are fully wilted, 2 to 3 minutes, then transfer them to the colander. When they're cool enough to handle, squeeze out the water from the greens with your hands, then roughly chop them and set them aside in a large mixing bowl.

Working in the same sauté pan that you used to cook the greens, add the last tablespoon of olive oil and the mushrooms and bring the heat to medium. Cook the mushrooms until they are tender, then remove them to the colander, squeezing out their water with your hands when they are cool enough to handle.

Roughly chop the mushrooms, add them to the bowl with the greens, then add the ricotta, lemon zest, and nutmeg. Stir to combine and season liberally with salt and pepper. Set aside or refrigerate until it is time to fill the ravioli.

Follow the instructions on page 48 to roll out the pasta dough into thin sheets, about 4 inches by 3 feet (10 by 91.5 cm). Lightly flour the sheets and cut them in half. Flour your work surface, and lay out one pasta sheet horizontally.

Brush the long edges of the sheet with the egg and add 1-tablespoon portions of filling 1 inch (2.5 cm) apart, leaving ½ inch (12 mm) border at each end. Top with a second sheet of pasta, then gently press down between the filling where you will cut it, making sure there are no bubbles. Cut the ravioli where you pressed down with a sharp knife or fluted pastry wheel.

Cook the pasta: Oil a baking sheet or line it with parchment paper. Bring a large pot of well-salted water to a boil. Cook the ravioli in small batches, scooping them onto the baking sheet with a slotted spoon when they are just al dente, about 1½ minutes. Reserve 1 cup (240 ml) of the pasta cooking water.

Make the sauce: In a large skillet, big enough to hold all the ravioli, carefully heat 4 tablespoons (55 g) of the butter over medium to medium-high heat until it begins to turn brown and take on a nutty smell. Turn off the heat, add the hot pasta cooking water, then swirl in the remaining 4 tablespoons (55 g) of cold butter until it melts.

Add the ravioli, thyme, and lemon zest, then turn the heat back up to low. Gently toss the ravioli in the butter to warm them and cover them with the sauce. Serve as soon as they are heated through, sprinkled with cheese and black pepper.

LAMB RAGU

with *fresh fettuccine*

SERVES 6 TO 10

This sauce is so delicious, you'll want to eat it by the bowlful (in testing it for this book, we did). You could generously serve six people with this recipe and still have some left over, or you could stretch the sauce to serve ten. I love a ragu—it's like the original sloppy Joe. I eat it on bread and in a bowl. I'd always make a huge pot at home, then toss it with some pasta to feed a gazillion people. Like anchovies, the cocoa powder gives a depth of flavor to the dish—you won't taste it, but it makes all the difference. You could also finish this sauce with cream, add tomato paste or ground chicken livers, or make it with wild boar instead of lamb. I've found that it tastes better if you puree the tomatoes yourself, rather than buying a puree, and I also prepare this with the fettuccine made from the recipe on page 47, but store-bought pasta is fine; just use a good-quality one to stand up to this sauce.

TIP *Always keep the rinds from your aged cheeses. They can add so much flavor to soups and stocks and ragus like this one. You can also just cut the rind off a new chunk for this recipe—it'll be fine.*

FOR THE RAGU

2	sprigs fresh thyme
	Peel from 1 lemon, pith removed
2-	to 3-inch (5- to 7.5-cm) piece Parmigiano-Reggiano cheese rind, scrubbed clean
2 1/2	pounds (1.2 kg) ground lamb
2 3/4	cups (350 g) finely diced onions
2 1/2	cups (215 g) finely diced carrots
1	leek, white and pale green parts, cut into small dice
2	tablespoons minced garlic
2	anchovy fillets, rinsed and dried
2	tablespoons tomato paste
2	cups (480 ml) red wine
1	can (28 ounces/794 g) whole peeled tomatoes, pureed
1	box (26.46 ounces/750 g) diced tomatoes
1	tablespoon unsweetened cocoa powder
1	tablespoon kosher salt, plus extra for seasoning
	Freshly ground black pepper

FOR THE PASTA

1	batch fresh pasta dough (page 47), prepared as fettuccine
1/2	cup (1 stick/115 g) unsalted butter, cut into 8 uniform pieces
	Freshly grated Parmigiano-Reggiano cheese, for garnish

RECIPE FOLLOWS

Make the ragu: Bundle the thyme, lemon peel, and cheese rind in a piece of cheesecloth tied with kitchen twine and set aside.

Heat a large heavy-bottomed pot over high heat until you can feel the heat when you hold your hand over the pan. Add the lamb and break the meat up into small pieces with a wooden spoon or spatula. Cook until the lamb is evenly browned on all sides, stirring occasionally, about 7 minutes. Using a slotted spoon, remove the meat to a bowl and set it aside.

Add the onions, carrots, leek, and garlic to the pot with the lamb juices and fat, and reduce the heat to medium-high. Cook until the vegetables are soft, about 5 minutes. A little brown "fond," or crust forming on the bottom of the pan is fine; just don't let it blacken.

Add the anchovies and tomato paste and cook, stirring, until the anchovies break down into the sauce, usually less than a minute. Add the wine and simmer the mixture until it reduces by half, about 7 minutes.

Return the lamb to the pot with the pureed and diced tomatoes. Add the bundle of thyme, lemon peel, and rind, making sure it's covered by the sauce. Sprinkle the cocoa powder over the sauce (making sure it doesn't clump) and stir it in. Add the salt and simmer the sauce gently for 1 hour, loosely covered with a lid so steam can escape but the sauce doesn't thicken much. Remove the cheesecloth bundle and discard. Season the ragu with salt and pepper and set it aside to cool until you're ready to cook the pasta. You can cover and refrigerate it for up to 1 week or freeze it for up to 1 month.

Cook the pasta: Bring a large pot of well-salted water to a boil and cook the pasta until it is just al dente, about 1½ minutes. Reserve ¼ cup (120 ml) of the pasta cooking water, then drain the pasta and set it aside.

Meanwhile, reheat the sauce gently over medium heat in another large pot. When it is hot, stir in the butter and the reserved pasta water. Toss the pasta with the sauce and serve it immediately, sprinkled with the cheese.

PORK AND CHIVE DUMPLINGS

with *dipping sauce*

MAKES ABOUT 100 DUMPLINGS

Once you are on a national TV show called *Throwdown with Bobby Flay*, and you best him with these dumplings, whatever culinary fame you aspired to is gone, and you are forever known as the Dumpling Lady. It's an honor I will cherish forever—especially if it helps to get picky eaters like my kids to eat their dinner. I put these dumplings on my opening menu, but never did I intend to keep them on for a decade. There's no getting rid of them now: These dumplings are the most popular item with some of our customers, including kids of all ages. In my opinion, dumplings are one of those perfect foods that are soulful, flavorful, and comforting. Another great thing about dumplings is that you can use practically anything in the filling—and you can pan-fry them, which is what we do, or boil or deep-fry them. These particular dumplings are a hybrid of Japanese *gyoza* (with the thin wrapper), Korean *mandoo* (the use of pork, chives, and tofu, which makes them silky and less like meatballs), and Chinese dumplings (with hoisin and dark soy sauce). I add the hoisin, which I like to joke is Chinese ketchup, because it makes these dumplings a touch sweeter. I think it is actually why people go crazy for them, because the American palate craves sweet and salty. This filling also makes an awesome breakfast patty, or put it on a bun with kimchee slaw for a great pork burger slider!

> **TIP** *I learned how to fold dumplings at an early age with the help of my grandmother and mother, and before we opened The Good Fork, I used to have dumpling-making parties at home. That's how I know that making one hundred dumplings at a time sounds daunting but is the only way to do it. Gather a few friends, make the dumplings together, then you each get some to tuck away—packaged by the dozen—into the freezer for weeks to come.*

Canola oil

1	large onion, finely diced
5	large cloves garlic, minced
2	tablespoons minced peeled fresh ginger
1 1/2	cups (85 g) finely chopped Chinese garlic chives, scallions, or regular chives
1	cup (250 g) crumbled soft tofu
1/3	to 1/2 cup (75 to 120 ml) hoisin sauce
1	teaspoon kosher salt, plus more if needed
1/4	teaspoon freshly ground black pepper
2	pounds (910 g) ground pork
2	packages (14 ounces/396 g each) thin or gyoza-style dumpling wrappers

Dumpling Dipping Sauce (recipe follows)

RECIPE FOLLOWS

In a large sauté pan, heat 2 teaspoons oil over medium heat and sauté the onion, garlic, and ginger until translucent and slightly caramelized. Add the chives and cook just to soften them, about 1 minute longer. Transfer the mixture to a large bowl and let it cool.

Once the onion has cooled, add the tofu, ⅓ cup (75 ml) of the hoisin sauce, the salt, and pepper and mix well. Add the pork to the bowl and mix it with the seasonings until you can see that the chives and tofu are evenly distributed throughout the meat.

In a small frying pan, cook a small spoonful of the meat mixture in a little bit of oil. Taste and adjust the seasoning of the meat with more hoisin sauce and/or salt, if necessary.

Prepare a small dish of water and line several baking sheets with parchment paper. Place about 1 tablespoon of filling in each dumpling wrapper. Using your finger, paint a little water around the edge of the wrapper. Fold the wrapper in half and simply pinch it closed, or crimp it following the photographs on pages 61–62. Place each finished dumpling on the baking sheet and repeat until you've used all the filling.

You can freeze them directly on the baking sheet until they harden, then pack them into plastic freezer bags. (They do not refrigerate well.) They will last for 3 months.

To cook fresh or frozen dumplings (see Note), heat a nonstick frying pan or well-seasoned cast-iron skillet with just enough oil to coat the bottom. Add just enough dumplings so that they are not overcrowded and don't touch. Brown the dumplings on one side, then add about ¼ inch (6 mm) of water, cover, and steam the dumplings until nearly all the water evaporates.

Remove the cover and let the dumplings begin to fry again, just long enough to crisp them slightly, then serve them immediately with the dipping sauce.

NOTE *To cook frozen dumplings, follow the same procedure above for fresh dumplings, but use ⅓ inch (8 mm) water so they steam a little longer and cook through.*

DUMPLING DIPPING SAUCE

MAKES ABOUT 1 CUP (240 ML)

¼   cup (120 ml) dark soy sauce
¼   cup (120 ml) rice wine vinegar
¼   cup (55 g) packed brown sugar
1   star anise pod

In a small saucepan, stir together the soy sauce, vinegar, brown sugar, and star anise and bring them to a simmer over medium-high heat, stirring so that the sugar dissolves. Once it does, remove the pot from the heat and let the mixture cool. Discard the star anise before serving.

This sauce keeps well in the refrigerator indefinitely and can also be multiplied, though you'll want to start with slightly less vinegar and adjust to taste.

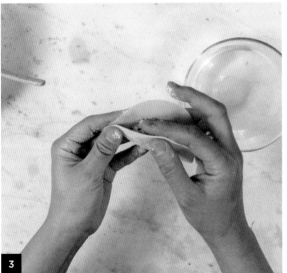

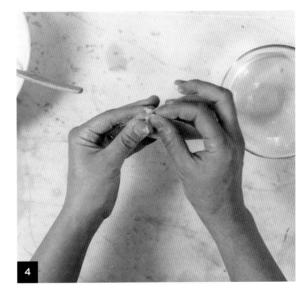

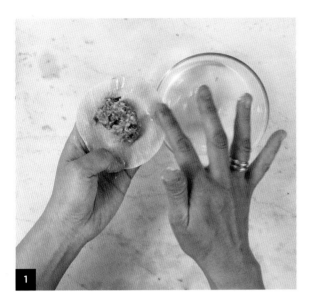

STEP 1.
Dab a bit of water around the edge of the wrapper.

STEP 2.
Make sure to center the meat filling and bring up half of wrapper as if to fold in half.

STEP 3.
Pinch to close the left end.

STEP 4.
With your right hand, push a little bit of wrapper into your fingertips of left hand and pinch it closed.

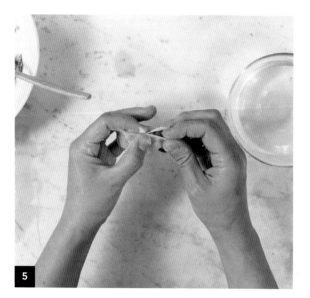

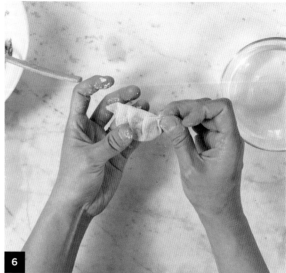

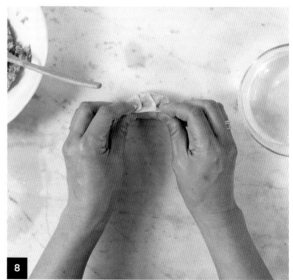

STEP 5.
Give a little pinch to
close the crimp.

STEP 6.
Four crimps should
do the trick.

STEP 7.
Make sure to press
firmly to seal it tight.

STEP 8.
With the crimps on
one side, smooth the
other side to make a
"purse."

VEGETABLE DUMPLINGS

WITH *dipping sauce*

MAKES ABOUT 100 DUMPLINGS

This is my number one way to get kids to eat vegetables! This healthy—actually vegan—snack uses what's in season and really brings out the sweetness of the vegetables. Unlike the Pork and Chive Dumplings (page 59), you get the crisp dumpling texture without all that fat. It's also a good way to use up things that are about to turn, such as that bag of CSA vegetables in the corner of the fridge screaming for your attention. Use this recipe as a guide to make up your own fillings with whatever is on hand. I also think these dumplings illustrate how to cook vegetables properly. Cooking each vegetable separately is really important here because they can contain a lot of water. For successful dumplings, you will want to cook some of the moisture out of them without overcooking them, and that's only possible if you deal with each vegetable on its own terms.

> **TIP** *In the summer, when vegetables are at their prime, they'll need very little seasoning. In the winter, the vegetables might need a little help, and you can use Mae Ploy sweet chili sauce to perk up their flavor.*

1	pound (455 g) fresh cremini or shiitake mushrooms
2	medium carrots
½	medium head green or Savoy cabbage
1	bunch Swiss chard
1	large onion
9	to 10 ounces (255 to 280 g) soft or silken tofu
5	tablespoons (75 ml) canola oil, plus extra for cooking
6	cloves garlic, minced
6	tablespoons (75 g) minced peeled fresh ginger
	Kosher salt
1	tablespoon hoisin sauce
1	teaspoon Thai sweet chili sauce (Mae Ploy, optional)
2	packages (14 ounces/393 g each) thin or gyoza-style dumpling wrappers
	Vegetable Dumpling Dipping Sauce (recipe follows) or Dumpling Dipping Sauce (page 60)

RECIPE FOLLOWS

Using a food processor, knife, or grater, finely dice or shred the vegetables individually and set them aside in separate bowls. Rinse the tofu, and set it on a paper towel–lined plate to drain.

Heat two large skillets or heavy-bottomed pans over medium-high heat. When you can feel the heat radiating from the pans, add 1 tablespoon of the oil to each; give it a few seconds to heat through, then add a little of the garlic and ginger to each pan and cook for about 30 seconds, or until you can smell them cooking. Put the carrots in one pan and the mushrooms in the other. Cook, stirring just enough to keep each from burning, until each is tender and slightly browned and the pan is dry. Transfer the cooked vegetables to one large mixing bowl, season to taste with salt, and set them aside.

In the same pans, repeat the process with the cabbage and chard: Add 1 tablespoon of the oil and half of the remaining garlic and ginger to each pan as before, then put the chard in one pan and the cabbage in the other. The chard will finish quickly; cook it just until it's tender and the pan is dry. Cook the cabbage until it is soft and a little browned. When they are done, transfer each to the bowl with the mushrooms and carrots.

Last, sauté the onion in the remaining 1 tablespoon oil until it is completely translucent, soft, and browned in a few spots. Add it to the other vegetables.

Once all the vegetables are cooked, place them together in a fine-mesh colander set over a bigger bowl, and let the mixture drain out excess moisture for at least 1 hour or up to overnight in fridge, covered. Do it by feel; it shouldn't be sticky or sopping wet.

As the vegetables drain, crumble the tofu into a large bowl. Add the cooked and drained vegetables and mix them together. Season with the hoisin, salt, and Thai sweet chili sauce.

Prepare a small dish of water and line several baking sheets with parchment paper. Place about 1 tablespoon of filling in each dumpling wrapper. Using your finger, paint a little water around the edge of the wrapper. Fold the wrapper in half and simply pinch it closed, or crimp it following the photographs on pages 61–62. Place each finished dumpling on the baking sheet and repeat until you've used all the filling.

You can freeze them directly on the baking sheet until they harden, then pack them into plastic freezer bags. (They do not refrigerate well.) They will last for 3 months.

To cook fresh or frozen dumplings (see Note), heat a nonstick frying pan or well-seasoned cast-iron skillet with just enough canola oil to coat the bottom. Add just enough dumplings so that they are not overcrowded and don't touch. Brown the dumplings on one side, then add about ¼ inch (6 mm) water, cover, and steam until nearly all the water evaporates.

Remove the cover and let the dumplings begin to fry again, just long enough to crisp them slightly, then serve them immediately with the Vegetable Dumpling Dipping Sauce or Dumpling Dipping Sauce.

NOTE *To cook frozen dumplings, follow the same procedure above for fresh dumplings, but use ⅓ inch (8 mm) water so they steam a little longer and cook through.*

VEGETABLE DUMPLING DIPPING SAUCE

MAKES ABOUT ¼ CUP (60 ML)

This will be enough for 20 to 25 vegetable dumplings. It can also be multiplied, though you'll want to start with slightly less vinegar and adjust to taste. Unlike the pork dumpling dipping sauce, this sauce won't keep indefinitely, so you don't want to make too much of it at a time.

1	tablespoon soy sauce
1	teaspoon vinegar
1	teaspoon brown sugar
	Pinch sesame seeds
¼	teaspoon thinly sliced scallions

In a small bowl, whisk together the soy sauce, vinegar, brown sugar, sesame seeds, scallions, and 1 teaspoon water.

FLOURLESS CHOCOLATE CAKE

MAKES 12 TO 16 INDIVIDUAL CAKES

As you'll no doubt learn by the time you reach the end of this book, I am not a dessert person. I'm Korean—a piece of fruit is dessert enough for me. My ideal is that and some dark chocolate. I do love chocolate. That's why this is my go-to, at-home dessert. It's fairly easy, but simple, elegant, and very, very chocolatey. Serve this with whipped cream or caramel sauce.

- 1 pound (455 g) unsalted butter, plus more for greasing the pans
- ¼ cup (25 g) unsweetened cocoa powder, plus more for dusting the pans
- 18 ounces (510 g) 60 to 70% bittersweet chocolate, chopped
- 10 large eggs
- 1 cup (200 g) sugar
- 1 teaspoon kosher salt
- Hot water

Preheat the oven to 425°F (220°C). Grease the cups of a cupcake pan or a set of sixteen 4-ounce (60-ml) ramekins with butter and dust them with cocoa powder. You will also need a large baking or roasting pan to fill with water for a water bath.

Over a double boiler with simmering water, melt together the chocolate and butter, then set the mixture aside.

In the bowl of an electric mixer fitted with a whisk attachment, whip together the eggs, sugar, and salt until they are fluffy and pale and drop in ribbons when you lift up the whisk.

Using a rubber spatula, stir a quarter of the chocolate mixture into the egg mixture. Add the rest of the chocolate mixture, and gently fold it in. Sift in the cocoa powder and then fold it into the batter.

Fill the cups or ramekins two-thirds full and place them in the baking pan. Pour in just enough hot water to reach halfway up the sides of the cups. Bake until the cakes are mostly set but still a little wobbly in the center, about 13 minutes.

Remove the ramekins from the water bath and let them cool for 10 minutes, then run a butter knife around the edge of each cake to loosen it before tipping them out of the pans. Serve them warm.

Refrigerate the cakes for up to 2 days, or freeze for up to 1 month. Reheat them in the oven before serving.

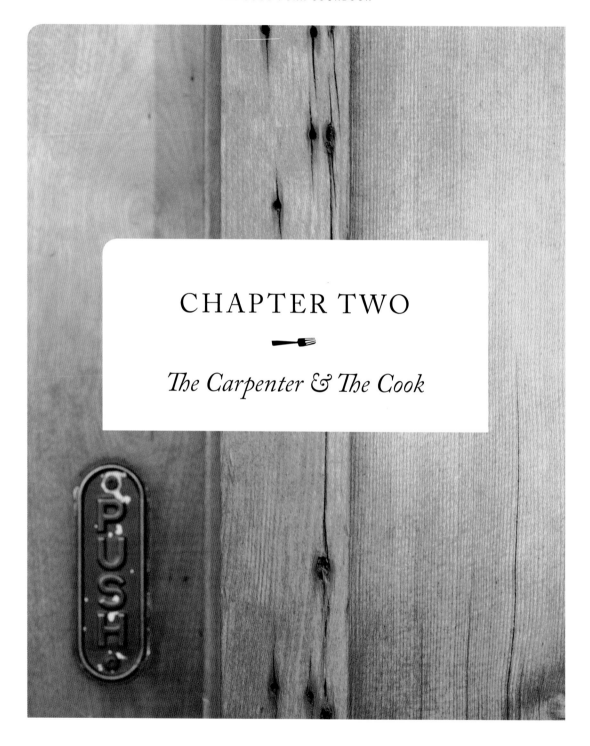

CHAPTER TWO

The Carpenter & The Cook

ONE EVENING ABOUT A DECADE AGO, Ben was down at Bait & Tackle, one of our favorite local watering holes in Red Hook, when a New York City Transit bus driver named Manny came in for a drink after his shift. He told Ben he'd been planning to open a deli in a building up the street, but now that he had this great city job, he didn't want to do it anymore. So Ben and Manny got up from the bar and headed right down the block—that is Ben in a nutshell—and went to look at this half-built store.

At the time, there weren't many places of any kind to eat in Red Hook, and Ben and I had always jokingly talked about opening a restaurant right in our own neighborhood. But we were always *joking*. Plus, I had the rare nine-to-five job as a cook, and Ben's acting career was going fairly well at the time. Despite all that—and despite the fact that the unfinished deli was a small space with low ceilings and little else of appeal—as soon as we saw it, we had a vision for what it could become.

And then we had to open a restaurant. And that meant I had to create a menu.

In reality, my personal cooking style is kind of globe-trotting—I take influences from all the things I like—but most people like to say my menu is Korean-fusion or modern Korean. That may be because some of those influences are obvious in the dishes we served during our opening weeks, which have gone on to become my signatures. For example, the Korean-style Steak and Eggs with Kimchee Fried Rice (page 94). But then and now, our menu reflects global inspiration, which most definitely goes beyond the perimeters of modern Korean. What was more important back then was that I wanted to serve what Ben and I wanted to eat. That meant not just the stuff we liked to make at home or for parties, but what we'd order when we went out to eat at our favorite neighborhood restaurants—the kind of restaurants we wanted ours to be.

That is why my very first menu—the recipes in this chapter—are exactly that; things I loved then and still love, like fried sweetbreads with watercress and grapefruit, gnocchi with mushrooms and peas, risotto, chocolate bread pudding, lots of lentil salads, and bright, compelling flavors from Korea and other parts of Asia, and my Soy-braised Short Ribs (page 100). Many of these are things I just can't take off the menu, no matter how many years go by.

"TONKATSU" SWEETBREAD SALAD

WITH *braised endive, watercress,* AND *grapefruit*

SERVES 6 TO 8

I love the rich flavor of sweetbreads—I order them whenever I see them—and when I opened The Good Fork, I *had* to have them on the menu, despite the fact that ten years ago they weren't as popular as they are now. I was thinking about Japanese *tonkatsu*, where meat, usually pork, is breaded in panko then deep-fried until a golden-brown crust forms; it's served with a thick, sweet sauce (kind of the Japanese version of HP Sauce). That's what I did to my sweetbreads, and then to cut the fattiness, I added grapefruit segments and stalks of watercress for a peppery bite. Of course the other star of the show here is the braised endive, inspired by a dish my mother-in-law, Jane, makes. I also used aged balsamic vinegar instead of the traditional tonkatsu sauce, to give it a little more contrast. If you don't want to invest in the aged balsamic vinegar, which is expensive, you can use *vincotto* or simply reduce regular balsamic vinegar in a small saucepan until it thickens (see page 29).

> TIP *I prefer to break my sweetbreads apart into smaller 2-inch (5-cm) nuggets by hand, cleaning off any large pieces of membrane and veins as I do. The shape is more organic, and they'll look and taste cleaner, too.*

FOR THE SWEETBREADS

- 1 pound (455 g) cleaned sweetbreads
  Milk for soaking
- 2 tablespoons kosher salt
- 1/2 cup (65 g) all-purpose flour
- 2 large eggs, beaten until frothy
- 1 1/4 cups (120 g) panko
  Freshly ground black pepper
  Canola oil, for frying

FOR THE BRAISED ENDIVE

- 3 tablespoons extra-virgin olive oil
- 4 Belgian endives, halved lengthwise
- 1 sprig fresh thyme
- 6 tablespoons (90 ml) dry vermouth
  or white wine
- 1 teaspoon sugar
- 1 1/2 cups (480 ml) chicken stock
- 1 1/2 teaspoons salt
- 1 tablespoon cold unsalted butter

FOR THE SALAD

- 1 bunch watercress or upland cress,
  tough stems removed
- 1 medium grapefruit
- 2 tablespoons aged or reduced balsamic
  vinegar or vincotto

RECIPE FOLLOWS

Make the sweetbreads: Put the sweetbreads in a medium-size bowl and cover them with milk. Add the salt and refrigerate for at least 3 hours or up to overnight.

To prepare the sweetbreads, set a wire rack on a clean baking sheet and measure the flour, eggs, and panko into three separate bowls. Rinse off the sweetbreads in cold water and pat them dry. Using a pair of kitchen scissors, trim the membrane, holding the sections of sweetbread together in order to cut or pull them into 2-inch (5-cm) hunks. Sprinkle the pieces on all sides with salt and pepper. Dredge each piece first in the flour, shaking off any excess, then dip it in the beaten eggs and coat it in the panko, setting it on the rack to dry for at least 10 minutes.

Set a clean wire rack on another baking sheet. Heat 1 inch (2.5 cm) of canola oil in a wide frying pan over medium-high heat until it begins to shimmer. Using tongs, slowly place each piece of sweetbread in the oil, holding them away from you to avoid any splatter. Fry them until golden brown on both sides, 2 to 2½ minutes per side. Let them cool slightly on the rack while making the endive and assembling the salad.

Make the braised endive: In a skillet large enough to hold all the endive, heat the olive oil over medium heat. When the oil begins to shimmer, place the endives in the pan, cut side down. When the bottoms are golden brown, flip the endives over, add the thyme, and brown the other sides. Add the vermouth, stirring to loosen any bits on the bottom of the pan, sprinkle the sugar over the endives, and then simmer until the vermouth evaporates.

Flip the endive over, cut side down, and add the stock and salt. Bring the stock to a low boil and cook until it is reduced by at least half, 12 to 15 minutes. Reduce the heat to low and swirl in the butter until the sauce emulsifies. Remove from the heat and set aside.

Cut the grapefruit into "supremes" as follows: Slice the top and bottom off the fruit, just deep enough to reveal the flesh. Place the fruit on a cutting board with one of the sliced sides facing down. Using a paring knife, carve away the skin, pith, and membrane from top to bottom, revealing the flesh. Hold the naked grapefruit in one hand, and with the other, carefully slice each segment out of the membrane into a bowl, collecting any juices. These are your supremes. Set aside.

Serve the salad: Scatter the cress on the bottom of a large serving platter and arrange the endive evenly over the top. Do the same with the grapefruit supremes and sweetbreads. Drizzle the braised endive sauce over the salad, then sprinkle on the reduced balsamic vinegar and serve immediately.

LONG BEAN SALAD

WITH *coconut–lime vinaigrette*

SERVES 4 TO 6

This salad was perfected slowly over time, as it was something of a personal mission. In fact, Ben hated it at first. "This is weird," was his initial verdict. But following my "serve what I like to eat" mantra, I kept working on it until I hit on this combination. It might be a little unconventional, but that's what I like about it. I love beans in general, but Chinese long beans are so dramatic. It might seem daunting to blanch them whole instead of cutting them up into bite-size pieces, but that's part of the appeal of this salad—people just twirl them up with their forks like spaghetti. I also think it's nice to serve a dish or a salad that doesn't have leafy greens but instead crisp vegetables and an in-your-face coconut-lime vinaigrette that holds everything together.

TIP *Most of this salad can be made several hours ahead. Just place the blanched beans, grapefruit supremes, sliced radishes, and sliced endive in separate containers, submerging the sliced radishes and endive in cold water to keep them from browning. Cover each container and refrigerate.*

FOR THE **COCONUT-LIME VINAIGRETTE**

- 1/4 cup (60 ml) liquid coconut oil
- 2 tablespoons coconut milk
- 1 tablespoon Mae Ploy Thai sweet chili sauce
- 2 tablespoons Dijon mustard
- 1 1/2 teaspoons fish sauce
- 1 teaspoon soy sauce
- 1 lime, zested and juiced

FOR THE **SALAD**

- Kosher salt
- 2 pounds (910 g) long beans, cleaned and trimmed
- 1 medium grapefruit
- 1 bunch Easter radishes, sliced into thin rounds
- 1 Belgian endive, sliced lengthwise into 1/4-inch (6-mm) strips
- 1/4 cup (20 g) unsweetened shaved coconut, toasted, or roasted chopped peanuts (35 g)
- 1 packed cup (50 g) fresh herb leaves, such as mint and Thai basil

RECIPE FOLLOWS

Make the dressing: In a jar with a lid, combine the coconut oil, coconut milk, sweet chili sauce, mustard, fish sauce, soy sauce, lime zest, and lime juice. Shake vigorously to combine.

Make the salad: Bring a large pot of well-salted water to a boil and fill a large bowl with salted water and ice. Blanch the beans in the boiling water for 3 minutes, or until they are bright green and barely tender, then submerge them in the ice water until they have cooled. Drain the beans and put them in a large salad bowl.

Cut the grapefruit into "supremes" as follows: Slice the top and bottom off the fruit, just deep enough to reveal the flesh. Place the fruit on a cutting board with one of the sliced sides facing down. Using a paring knife, carve away the skin, pith, and membrane from top to bottom, revealing the flesh. Hold the naked grapefruit in one hand, and with the other, carefully slice each segment out of the membrane into a bowl, collecting any juices. These are your supremes. Set aside.

Add the sliced radishes and endive to the salad bowl and drizzle most of the dressing over the vegetables, tossing to coat evenly. Add more dressing to taste, then arrange the supremes and their juices on top of the vegetables, sprinkle the coconut pieces and herbs over the top, and serve immediately.

MUSSELS

WITH *lime leaf, coconut milk,* AND *lemongrass*

SERVES 4 TO 6

I could taste this dish in my head before I created it. I'm a huge fan of Thai and Vietnamese food, and I wanted the flavors of a Thai curry—chiles, the smoothness of coconut milk, lemongrass, kaffir lime—in the broth for my mussels. I tried it for staff meal: so good. At first I wasn't sure if the coconut milk would go with wine, but once I reduced the mixture, not only did it work, it made the coconut milk less cloying. It's just like making a French sauce, where you use levels of reduction to build complexity, rather than throwing the mussels and wine in all at the same time. Best yet, it takes only ten minutes more for a lot more flavor. In fact, mussels are actually the easiest things to prepare. Serve this with a slab of grilled bread slathered with Sriracha Aioli (page 38)—French bistro style—to sop up the broth. Or maybe do it Belgian style, with French fries!

2	pounds (910 g) fresh mussels
1	tablespoon canola oil
1	large shallot, thinly sliced
1	clove garlic, minced
1	can (13.5 ounces/385 g) unsweetened coconut milk
1	cup (240 ml) white wine
1	stalk lemongrass, bottom third only, thinly sliced
1	or 2 small Thai bird's eye chiles, seeded and finely chopped
2	large or 3 small kaffir lime leaves, thinly sliced
	Kosher salt and freshly ground black pepper
1	tablespoon chopped fresh cilantro leaves, plus extra for garnish

Thoroughly wash the mussels, debeard them if necessary, and discard any with shells that are unopened or cracked.

In a large pot with a lid, heat the oil over medium heat. Add the shallot and garlic and sauté, stirring occasionally, until they are translucent and fragrant.

Add the coconut milk, white wine, lemongrass, 1 or 2 chiles (depending on how spicy you want the broth to be), and kaffir lime leaves to the shallot and garlic. Turn the heat to high and simmer for about 10 minutes, until the liquid thickens.

Season the simmering mixture with salt and pepper to taste, then add the chopped cilantro and the mussels. Cover the pot and check the mussels after they have cooked for 2 minutes, removing them to a clean bowl as soon as they open. Once all are open (discarding any that do not open), serve them in one large or individual bowls with their broth, garnished with more chopped cilantro or whole sprigs.

BROILED WHOLE SARDINES

WITH *warm red lentil salad* AND *pickled fennel, apple,* AND *radishes*

SERVES 4

Red lentils are very sweet and easily fall apart when they're cooked, which I found out early on after The Good Fork opened. But I turned that stressful mistake into a nifty salad that was a great accompaniment to salty grilled sardines. The fennel-apple-radish pickles that top it off are my riff on the sweet pickled daikon that you get with Korean fried chicken. They are very easy to make and, like the daikon, are crisp, tart, and sweet, a nice pairing with anything fatty, fried, or barbecued. They also work well chopped up into a slaw. Note that I often use the Korean radish called *moo* instead of the similar daikon if I can find it, and you can, too.

> **TIP** *You will make your life much easier if you have your fishmonger scale, gut, and clean the sardines for you. If not, sardine scales luckily are small. Put the fish in a plastic supermarket bag and scrape the scales against the grain with a knife. Then use kitchen scissors to cut the fish lengthwise up the belly and remove the gills and guts. Just give them a quick wash under running water and pat them dry.*

FOR THE **PICKLES**

- 1 small fennel bulb, cored and cut into 2 by $1/4$-inch (5-cm by 6-mm) matchstick strips
- 6 ounces (170 g) daikon radish or *moo*, peeled and cut into 2 by $1/4$-inch (5-cm by 6-mm) matchstick strips
- 1 cup (240 ml) white distilled vinegar
- $1/4$ cup (50 g) sugar
- 1 tablespoon kosher salt
- 1 Granny Smith apple, cored and cut into 2 by $1/4$-inch (5-cm by 6-mm) matchstick strips

FOR THE **RED LENTIL SALAD**

- 1 cup (200 g) red lentils, rinsed and picked through
- 4 tablespoons (60 ml) extra-virgin olive oil
- 1 cup (125 g) finely diced onion
- $1/2$ cup (70 g) finely diced carrot
- 2 cloves garlic, minced
- $1/2$ cup (120 ml) chicken stock
- $1/4$ teaspoon gochujaru (Korean red chile flakes; see page 21) or another dried red chile flake
- 3 tablespoons sherry wine vinegar
- 2 tablespoons chopped fresh parsley, plus extra leaves for garnish
- 1 $1/4$ teaspoons kosher salt

  Freshly ground black pepper

FOR THE **SARDINES**

- 4 whole sardines, scaled, cleaned, and gutted
- 2 tablespoons extra-virgin olive oil

  Salt and freshly ground black pepper

RECIPE FOLLOWS

Make the pickles: In a bowl or 1-quart (960-ml) container, combine the fennel and radish. Combine 1 cup (240 ml) water with the vinegar, sugar, and salt in a pot. Bring to a boil, stirring to dissolve the sugar. Pour the hot vinegar mixture over the vegetables. Allow them to cool, then add the apple. This can be made up to a day in advance.

Make the salad: In a small pot, combine the lentils with enough water to cover by 1 inch (2.5 cm) and bring to a boil. Simmer for 6 to 8 minutes, until soft. Drain in a sieve and set aside.

In a medium saucepan, heat 1 tablespoon of the olive oil over medium-high heat and sauté the onion and carrot. When the onion becomes translucent, about 3 minutes, add the garlic. Continue to sauté until the mixture just begins

to brown, about 3 minutes more. Add the stock and chile flakes and simmer until the carrots are very soft, about 7 minutes.

Turn off the heat and fold in the lentils, vinegar, parsley, and the remaining 3 tablespoons olive oil. Season with the salt and pepper. Spread the salad on a platter.

Make the sardines: Position an oven rack in the middle of the oven, and preheat the broiler. Pat the sardines dry, and season them lightly with the olive oil, salt, and pepper.

Broil the sardines for about 6 minutes, turning them halfway through, until they are blistered on both sides.

To serve, place the sardines on top of the salad and garnish with the pickles and parsley leaves.

WATERMELON SALAD

WITH *kimchee-pickled rind, blue cheese,* AND *toasted sunflower seeds*

SERVES 4

To me, a good salad should be fresh and crunchy and have a kick-ass vinaigrette and an element of surprise. Here, that's provided by the kimchee-pickled watermelon rind—and a sprinkle of salted, toasted sunflower seeds. Kimchee goes with a lot of things one wouldn't expect, like the blue cheese in this salad. You can also use easier-to-find traditional daikon radish kimchee instead of making the watermelon rind and, in fact, that is what gave me the idea in the first place. I realized the rind was similar in texture to a daikon radish, so I threw it in some leftover kimchee brine for a couple of days. If you happen to have some brine sitting around, that's all you need to do, too, though I now usually make my kimchee-pickled watermelon rind from scratch.

FOR THE LIME VINAIGRETTE

1/4 cup (60 ml) fresh lime juice, or to taste

1/4 cup (60 ml) extra-virgin olive oil

3 tablespoons canola or grapeseed oil

1 teaspoon honey

1 teaspoon Dijon mustard

1/2 teaspoon kosher salt, or to taste

FOR THE SALAD

1 teaspoon extra-virgin olive oil

1/4 cup (30 g) sunflower seeds

Kosher salt

1 head frisée lettuce

3 cups (480 g) cubed watermelon

1 cup (160 g) cubed Kimchee-pickled Watermelon Rind (recipe follows) or daikon kimchee

1/4 cup (13 g) fresh flat-leaf parsley leaves

1/4 pound (115 g) Fourme d'Ambert or other sweet creamy blue cheese

Make the vinaigrette: In a jar with a lid, combine the lime juice, both oils, honey, mustard, and salt and seal the jar. Shake to combine. Adjust the seasoning with salt or lime juice to taste. (This will keep in the refrigerator for 2 to 3 days.)

Make the salad: In a skillet, heat the olive oil over medium heat. Toast the sunflower seeds in the hot oil until they smell nutty and begin to color slightly. Sprinkle them with a large pinch of salt and set aside.

In your largest mixing bowl, toss the frisée, watermelon, pickled rind, and parsley with just enough vinaigrette to coat the leaves. Transfer the salad to a serving platter or salad bowl. Roughly crumble the cheese on top and sprinkle the toasted sunflower seeds over the tossed salad; serve immediately.

KIMCHEE-PICKLED WATERMELON RIND

MAKES 6 CUPS (1.5 L)

	Rind from ¼ large watermelon, diced
¼	cup (32 g) kosher salt
¼	cup (50 g) sugar
⅓	cup (40 g) gochujaru (Korean dried red chile flakes; see page 21)
2	tablespoons minced garlic
1	to 2 tablespoons fish sauce
2	teaspoons minced peeled fresh ginger

Place the diced rind in a large nonreactive bowl. Sprinkle the salt and sugar over the rind, and let it stand at room temperature for at least 1 hour and up to 3 hours.

Toss the rind to evenly distribute any remaining sugar and salt. Strain off any standing water, reserving it for the seasoning paste.

In a small bowl, mix the chile flakes, garlic, fish sauce, and ginger. Add 3 tablespoons of the reserved water from the watermelon rind and stir to make a smooth paste.

Mix the paste into the watermelon rind, making sure to evenly coat the pieces, then transfer the mixture to a 1-quart (960-ml) container or jar. You can it eat right away, but the flavor improves after a day or two. I keep it out on the counter for 6 hours before storing it in the refrigerator, where it will keep for at least 3 weeks.

SUMMER SALAD

WITH *French feta* AND *kohlrabi*

SERVES 4

This is a simple end-of-summer salad that is extremely refreshing, with plenty of crunch. Its special ingredient is kohlrabi, one of those vegetables that friends always ask me about when it makes an appearance in their CSA bags. It's a broccoli relative, where the swollen stem is what you eat instead of the flower buds. You can serve kohlrabi raw or cooked—it has the mildly sweet flavor of a young cabbage or even broccoli stems. I created this salad because of an urban farm called Added Value that operates a few blocks away from us. When they first started, we tried to buy from them whenever we could. They built their growing beds on top of an old playground, so they could only grow things without deep root systems like lettuces, eggplant, and, of course, kohlrabi.

> TIP *A few notes on this salad's composition: I prefer to use French fetas over Greek varieties, because they are less salty. After you wash the lettuce in plenty of cold water, get it as dry as you can so that the dressing will cling to the leaves. You can also prepare all the ingredients for the salad in advance and then compose the dish just before serving. Just be sure to refrigerate the kohlrabi, cucumber, and watermelon in separate containers.*

FOR THE CITRUS-PICKLED RED ONIONS

¼	cup (60 ml) fresh lemon juice
¼	cup (60 ml) fresh lime juice
¼	cup (60 ml) fresh orange juice
1	small clove garlic, crushed
1	tablespoon kosher salt
½	teaspoon freshly ground black pepper
¾	teaspoon minced fresh oregano, or ¼ teaspoon dried
1	large red onion, sliced into ⅛-inch (3-mm) thick rings

FOR THE SHERRY WINE VINAIGRETTE

1	cup (240 ml) extra-virgin olive oil
½	cup (120 ml) canola oil
½	cup (120 ml) sherry wine vinegar
2	tablespoons honey
1½	teaspoons Dijon mustard

FOR THE SALAD

1	head oak leaf or butter lettuce, washed and well dried
½	medium bulb kohlrabi, peeled and cut into 2 by ¼-inch (5-cm by 6-mm) matchstick strips
½	English cucumber, cut into 2 by ¼-inch (5-cm by 6-mm) matchstick strips
3	cups (450 g) cubed watermelon
1	cup (150 g) crumbled feta cheese (see Tip)

Make the onions: In a bowl, whisk together the citrus juices, garlic, salt, pepper, and oregano. Pack the onion slices into a glass jar or nonreactive bowl and cover them with the brine. Refrigerate for at least 3 hours and up to 3 days.

Make the vinaigrette: In a small glass jar with a lid, combine the olive oil, canola oil, vinegar, honey, and mustard. Seal the jar and shake it hard until the vinaigrette emulsifies. Season to taste with salt and pepper, and then shake again to mix thoroughly; set aside until you make the salad.

Make the salad: In a large salad bowl, toss the lettuce, kohlrabi, cucumber, and one third of the pickled onions with 3 tablespoons of the vinaigrette. Add the watermelon and fold it in gently with your hands. In the serving bowl or on individual plates, compose the salad by bringing most of the watermelon pieces and onion rings to the top, or sprinkle 3 pickled onion rings over each plate, and then the cheese over the top. Serve immediately.

BRUSSELS SPROUTS CAESAR SALAD

WITH *maple bacon* AND *soft eggs*

SERVES 3 TO 4

This is one of Ben's favorite recipes. He loves the combination of two textures of Brussels sprouts— the roasted chunks and the blanched leaves—and also the true Caesar dressing made with salty anchovies. Plus, it has soft eggs and bacon. I love to use bacon as a cheat to make things taste better, and here I really pushed the envelope by glazing it with maple syrup. In fact, this is actually a very indulgent dish masquerading as a healthy one, because it's centered around those Brussels sprouts. That makes it a very good way to get those who don't like green vegetables (like my children and my husband) to eat them.

FOR THE **CAESAR DRESSING**

1/2	cup (50 g) freshly grated Parmigiano-Reggiano cheese
2	egg yolks
2	anchovy fillets, rinsed and patted dry
2	cloves garlic
1	tablespoon white wine vinegar
1	lemon, zested and juiced
2	teaspoons Worcestershire sauce
1/4	teaspoon kosher salt
3/4	cup (180 ml) canola oil
	Freshly ground black pepper

FOR THE **BRUSSELS SPROUTS SALAD**

1 1/4	pounds (570 g) Brussels sprouts
2	tablespoons extra-virgin olive oil
	Salt and freshly ground black pepper
5	strips thick-cut bacon, cut into 3/4-inch (2-cm) pieces
2	tablespoons maple syrup
2	large eggs
8	fresh chives, cut into 1-inch (2.5-cm) pieces

RECIPE FOLLOWS

Make the dressing: In a blender, combine the cheese, egg yolks, anchovies, garlic, vinegar, the lemon zest and juice, and Worcestershire sauce. Blend until smooth and season with the salt. With the blender running on high, slowly drizzle in the canola oil until it is completely emulsified. The dressing should be very thick. Gradually add up to ½ cup (120 ml) water to thin it out; it should be looser than mayonnaise, but thicker than vinaigrette.

Season with pepper and refrigerate until you prepare the salad. This will make 2 cups (480 ml) dressing that will keep, refrigerated, for up to 1 week.

Make the Brussels sprouts: Preheat the oven to 475°F (245°C) and place a clean baking sheet in the oven to warm. Trim the bottoms of half of the Brussels sprouts and quarter them lengthwise. In a large bowl, toss them with the olive oil and season with salt and pepper. Transfer them to the hot baking sheet and roast until they're golden brown, about 15 minutes, shaking the pan halfway through cooking to flip the Brussels sprouts. Set aside to cool.

Meanwhile, bring a large pot of salted water to a boil and fill a large work bowl with salted ice water. Cut the stems off the other half of the Brussels sprouts and separate the leaves. Blanch the leaves in the boiling salted water for 1½ minutes, until they are bright green and barely tender, then remove them immediately to the ice water. Drain and place them on a clean dish towel to dry.

In a large skillet over medium-high heat, cook the bacon until browned, about 8 minutes. Drain off the fat and add the maple syrup to the pan. Stir to coat the bacon; remove it from the heat and set aside. When it is cool, break it into pieces.

Bring a small pot of water to boil and fill a bowl or another pot with cold water with a \few ice cubes. Gently lower the eggs into the boiling water with a slotted spoon. Cook at a low boil for exactly 7 minutes. Remove the eggs to the cold water, then gently crack their shells; leave them submerged until completely cooled before peeling them and setting them aside.

Assemble the salad: In a large salad bowl, toss the roasted and blanched Brussels sprouts with ¼ cup (60 ml) of the dressing. Taste for salt and pepper. Transfer them to a serving plate and sprinkle with the bacon and chives. Slice the eggs in half and arrange them on the salad.

FRIED GREEN TOMATOES

WITH *jalapeño–citrus mayo*

SERVES 6

At the end of every growing year, our local farmers always have a large supply of phenomenal green tomatoes, which you have to eat before they can ripen or you'll lose them to the first frost. Fried ones are good, but it's really the citrus mayonnaise that makes this dish. Flavored mayos are a restaurant trick—you always have a bunch on hand to boost flavors here and there, and this one tastes clean and simple and bright. You will have extra mayonnaise, but it's hard to make any less because you need this proportion of oil to egg yolk to make it turn out properly—though who has any problem using up extra homemade mayo? For my tips on making it from scratch, see the recipe for Sriacha Aioli (page 38).

FOR THE **CITRUS MAYO**

1	egg yolk
2	teaspoons Dijon mustard
³/₄	cup (180 ml) canola oil
1	lime, zested and juiced
½	teaspoon kosher salt, or to taste
1	tablespoon minced canned pickled jalapeño
2	tablespoons canned pickled jalapeño juice, or to taste

FOR THE **TOMATOES**

6	large green (unripe) tomatoes
	Kosher salt and freshly ground black pepper
2	large eggs
²/₃	cup (80 g) all-purpose flour
3	cups (240 g) panko
	Canola or safflower oil, for frying

Make the citrus mayo: In a small bowl, whisk together the egg yolk and mustard. Add a few drops of oil at a time, whisking constantly. Continue whisking and add about half the oil in a slow trickle; the mixture should emulsify and stiffen and become thick and creamy.

Whisk in ½ teaspoon zest from the lime and all of its juice, then add the salt. Add the remainder of the oil in a thin, steady drizzle, whisking constantly, until you have used all the oil. Whisk in the jalapeño and pickled jalapeño juice. Add more salt or jalapeño juice to taste. Refrigerate until ready to use, up to 3 days.

Make the tomatoes: Slice the tomatoes ⅓ inch (8 mm) thick and lay them on paper towels. Sprinkle with salt and pepper. In a small bowl, beat the eggs until frothy. Spread out the flour on a plate or shallow bowl. Spread out the panko on another plate or shallow bowl. Place a wire cooling rack on a baking sheet. Dip both sides of a tomato slice in flour, then egg, then panko, and rest it on the wire rack. Repeat with all the tomatoes, then let the breading set for 5 minutes.

Heat ¼ inch (6 mm) of canola oil in a skillet over medium-high heat until the oil shimmers, about 2 minutes. Fry the tomatoes spaced at least 1 inch (2.5 cm) apart, working in batches if necessary, until they're golden brown, 60 to 90 seconds per side. Return the fried tomatoes to the wire rack to cool.

Serve them immediately with the citrus mayo.

GNOCCHI

WITH *sautéed mushrooms* AND *spring vegetables*

SERVES 4

Early on, I knew I wanted The Good Fork to also show off my love for Italian food, which I spent several years cooking professionally. I found that, like Korean food, it's simple, interesting, and soulful—I like to say that Koreans are the Italians of the East. Both cuisines are really about simplicity, and using the same short list of ingredients in different proportions to make so many different things. When it comes to pasta, I prefer homemade gnocchi over any other form, maybe because it reminds me of another love: Asian dumplings. Gnocchi is one of the simplest things you can make, but they're difficult to perfect, and I learn more about them every time I make them. Their texture should be puffy, cloud-like pillows, but with a bite, and to master that, timing is everything. You have to work quickly once the potatoes are cool enough to handle. If you wait too long and they cool completely, the dough will not bind properly. You'll also want to invest in a potato ricer, which is an inexpensive tool that is really key to giving your gnocchi proper texture. When we have it on the menu, we make gnocchi fresh every day at The Good Fork—two-day-old gnocchi are *no bueno*— and I often make them myself. (There has only been one cook thus far I have trusted with the task, and that's you, Dan Wollensky.) Just like pasta, fresh gnocchi can be paired with pretty much any sauce, and in this recipe, I let the flavor of the gnocchi shine with just a little help from beautiful spring vegetables.

TIP *You don't want to let gnocchi sit around, but I have found you can cook them up to 8 hours ahead. Cook them in boiling water for 1 to 2 minutes, then as soon as they float, submerge them in ice water to stop the cooking and to cool them rapidly. Drain them well, toss them with a touch of oil, and keep them in the refrigerator in a tightly sealed container until dinnertime, when you simply toss them in a pan with a touch of butter and your favorite sauce.*

FOR THE **GNOCCHI**

3   large russet potatoes, such as Idaho

3/4   cup (90 g) all-purpose flour, plus extra for dusting

1   large egg, beaten

1   tablespoon grated Parmigiano-Reggiano cheese

1 1/2   teaspoons kosher salt

1 1/2   tablespoons extra-virgin olive oil

FOR THE **SAUTÉ**

4   tablespoons (60 ml) extra-virgin olive oil

3   to 4 cups (180 to 240 g) thinly sliced fresh shiitake mushrooms

1   large shallot, minced

3   spring onions, thinly sliced on the bias

1 1/2   cups (220 g) spring peas, sugar snaps, peeled fava beans (see Note), or a mix
Freshly grated Parmigiano-Reggiano cheese
Freshly ground black pepper

Preheat the oven to 425°F (220°C).

Make the gnocchi: Wash the potatoes and prick them all over with a fork, then bake for 1 hour, or until the tines of a fork slide in easily and the potato gives a little when you press it with your finger. Flour a work surface, and while the potatoes are still hot, scoop out their flesh and pass it through a ricer—you can mash them or use a food mill, but it won't be quite the same—onto the flour.

Sprinkle the ¾ cup (90 g) flour over the riced potatoes, then do the same with the beaten egg, cheese, and salt. Fold them in and mix everything together with your hands, just until it holds together in a ball. It's ready when it feels light but it's not dense, and it springs back slightly to the touch.

Divide the dough into four pieces. Roll each out into a snake about ½ inch (12 mm) thick, then cut it into 1-inch (2.5-cm) pieces and set them aside on a floured surface. Don't be afraid to dust in more flour as you work if the dough is sticky.

Bring a large pot of lightly salted water to a boil, and boil the gnocchi until they float, 1 to 1½ minutes. Drain the gnocchi, reserving ¼ cup (60 ml) of the cooking liquid for the sauce, transfer them to a bowl or the empty pot, and toss with the extra-virgin olive oil. Set aside.

Make the sauté: In a large sauté pan, heat 2 tablespoons of the olive oil over medium heat. Sauté the mushrooms and shallots until the shallots are nearly translucent and the mushrooms are soft. Add the spring onions and peas and continue to sauté until everything is tender and warmed through, about 1 minute.

Toss the gnocchi with the sauté, adding the reserved cooking liquid and the remaining 2 tablespoons olive oil. Serve immediately, garnished with a sprinkle of cheese and pepper.

NOTE: *If you want to use fresh favas for this dish, you'll need about 2 pounds (910 g) of beans in their pods. Remove the beans from the pods and prepare a large bowl of ice water. Bring 1 quart (960 ml) of water to a boil in a large pot. Add the beans and boil for 1 to 2 minutes, until their skins pop off easily. Cool the fava beans in the ice bath, remove their skins, and set aside.*

FRENCH LENTIL AND SHREDDED DUCK SALAD

WITH *dried cherries* AND *piquillo peppers*

SERVES 4 TO 6

I believe this dish will convert anyone who thinks lentils are boring. They're nutty and creamy, have a great texture, and are good for you. Because they're often underutilized and tossed aside as a health food, I like to really do it up and let them shine. However, I'll admit the real reason I created this as a special—which is now one of my favorites—is that when I opened The Good Fork, I had lots of lentils because ordering grains in bulk was so much cheaper. This dish pairs amazingly with Seared Pekin Duck Breast (page 93) for a duck dinner two ways, which is how I serve it at the restaurant, but it's a fine meal on its own or just with a handful of salad greens tossed with Sherry Wine Vinaigrette (page 83). As far as the lentils go, French lentils, or *lentils du Puy*, are ideal, as they hold their shape and have great flavor.

> **TIP** *Though I love to make my own duck confit, many high-quality butcher shops and specialty food stores sell it today, or you can order it online. More importantly, you don't need the duck to make this salad: Like nearly any recipe I make that includes duck (which I love), you can easily substitute shredded chicken thighs or braised oxtails if you are so inclined, or even skip the meat altogether.*

1 cup (150 g) dried cherries or golden raisins
6 tablespoons (90 ml) red wine vinegar
2 packed cups (300 g) shredded duck confit (recipe follows)
1 pound (455 g) French lentils
1 teaspoon kosher salt, plus more for the salad
1 bay leaf
¼ cup (60 ml) extra-virgin olive oil
1 cup (150 g) diced, seeded canned piquillo peppers
2 small shallots, minced
½ cup (25 g) minced fresh chives
¼ cup (60 ml) warmed duck or bacon fat or extra-virgin olive oil
2 teaspoons Dijon mustard
   Freshly ground black pepper

In a small bowl, toss the cherries with the vinegar and set them aside to rehydrate. Bring the duck confit to room temperature if it has been refrigerated.

Rinse and pick through the lentils for stones or other detritus. Add the lentils to a large pot with 6 cups (1.4 L) water. Add the salt and the bay leaf and cook over medium-high heat until the lentils are tender but still firm—not mushy—about 20 minutes. Drain, transfer them to a large bowl, toss with the olive oil, and set aside.

Add the duck confit, piquillo peppers, shallots, chives, duck fat, mustard, and drained cherries to the lentils and toss to incorporate. Season well with salt and pepper.

Serve the salad warm or at room temperature with salad greens or Seared Pekin Duck Breast (page 93). This also keeps well, refrigerated, for up to 1 week.

DUCK CONFIT

MAKES 6 CUPS (750 G)

Duck confit, like the recipe for braising oxtails on page 177, is a great thing to have in your arsenal. Once you've mastered it, it's game on. You can put the meat in most everything you cook: salads, dumplings, spring rolls, hash...or just keep the legs whole in the fridge and then crisp up the skin for a Frenchy dinner on a Thursday night. The word *confit* generally refers to the idea of preserving something by cooking it in its own fat, which ensures that it will be rich, luxurious, and never dry. The aromatics provide deep flavor, and I sometimes add parsley stems and rosemary along with the thyme and bay leaf if I have them on hand. The preservation method actually begins with a salting process that takes about twenty-four hours—the rest is easy peasy.

8	skin-on duck legs
3	tablespoons kosher salt
10	cloves garlic
5	sprigs fresh thyme
2	bay leaves
1	tablespoon black peppercorns
3	to 4 cups (600 to 800 g) rendered duck fat

The day before you plan to cook the confit, place the duck legs in a baking dish and sprinkle the salt on both sides. Crush the garlic cloves with the side of a knife, then peel them and add them to the pan. Add the thyme, bay leaves, and peppercorns, then cover the dish and refrigerate it overnight.

The next day, preheat the oven to 275°F (135°C).

In a saucepan over medium heat, heat the duck fat until it melts. Pour the melted fat over the duck legs until they are well covered, then cover the dish with foil. Bake for 4 hours, or until the meat easily pulls away from the bone.

Let the duck legs cool to room temperature in the fat, then remove them and use. To store them for longer than a few days, tightly pack the duck legs into a container, and pour the melted but cooled fat over them. If the confit is completely covered by fat, it will keep well in the refrigerator for up to a few months.

SEARED PEKIN DUCK BREAST

WITH *port wine sauce, roasted plums,* AND *grilled scallions*

SERVES 2

This is a *wow* dish. It's both romantic and impressive. But it's only deceivingly fancy: The actual cooking of the dish is fairly simple. First, you make a nice little reduction sauce that's easier to get right than pot pie or lasagna. Meanwhile, you get a duck breast, score the skin, and render the fat; you can even start it in a cold pan. And save that fat! It's liquid gold, and I use it in my French Lentil and Shredded Duck Salad with Dried Cherries and Piquillo Peppers (page 91). Finally, pop it in a hot oven with the plums and scallions for about ten minutes. That's it! I suggest serving it with that amazing French lentil salad, as we did at The Good Fork, but it stands alone beautifully.

FOR THE PORT WINE SAUCE

2	quarts (2 L) chicken stock
2	cups (480 ml) red wine
1½	cups (360 ml) port wine
½	large onion, roughly chopped
1	medium carrot, peeled and roughly chopped
1	large shallot, peeled and halved
2	or 3 cloves garlic
2	sprigs fresh thyme

FOR THE DUCK BREAST

2	boneless, skin-on duck breasts
	Kosher salt and freshly ground black pepper
2	plums, halved and pitted
1	bunch scallions, trimmed

Make the sauce: In a saucepan, combine the stock, both wines, the onion, carrot, shallot, garlic, and thyme and bring to a boil. Boil the mixture until it reduces to a thick, syrupy sauce, about 40 minutes, watching it closely toward the end and stirring occasionally as it begins to thicken more quickly.

Strain out and discard the vegetables and aromatics, then set the sauce aside until you're ready to serve the dish.

Make the duck breast: Preheat the oven to 500°F (260°C). Score the duck skin, making a cross-hatch pattern, cutting through the fat to just shy of where it connects to the meat.

Sprinkle the breasts liberally with salt and pepper. In a skillet over medium-low heat, cook the duck, skin side down, until most of the fat has rendered and the skin has begun to brown, about 20 minutes. Pour the fat from the skillet, reserving it for another use. Working in the same skillet, turn the heat to high and cook the duck, skin side down, just until the skin of the duck begins to crisp.

Turn off the burner, add the plum halves and the scallions to the skillet, and transfer the pan to the oven. Roast until the duck is medium-rare (an internal temperature of 125 to 130°F/50 to 55°C), about 5 minutes.

Remove the duck from the pan and let it rest, skin side up, for at least 5 minutes before slicing it. If necessary, return the plums and scallions to the oven for another 5 to 10 minutes and cook them until they are soft.

To serve, reheat the port wine sauce if necessary, then slice the duck breasts and serve them topped with the plums, scallions, and port wine sauce.

KOREAN-STYLE STEAK AND EGGS

WITH *kimchee fried rice*

SERVES 4

This has become my signature dish over the years. We've been making it at The Good Fork since opening night. I never intended to continue doing that for nearly a decade, but try as I might, I can't take it off the menu. I came up with the idea largely because I wanted to do the kimchee fried rice I'd been making for years at home with bacon and eggs. If I added a steak, I realized, I'd have a twist on the American classic of steak and eggs. So I took my mother's traditional Korean *kalbi* beef marinade and tweaked it to be a little less sweet and a little more spicy. The mild sweet heat is just so delicious, especially with a hearty and flavorful piece of meat like skirt steak. In fact, the *New York Times* once wrote that it was "a lesson in how affordably priced restaurants should approach steak dishes." The kimchee fried rice itself is best made with day-old rice, and you can of course serve it as a stand-alone dish without the steak, as I do all the time at home. I usually make it with both day-old rice and the oldest, stinkiest kimchee sitting in the back of my fridge, and bring it all back to deliciousness by sautéing it in bacon fat with a little sugar and rice wine vinegar and mixing some crumbled cooked bacon in at the end. At the restaurant, I add the steak and top it all with a fried egg, just like you would serve *bibimbap*, the Korean sizzling rice bowl. So, to me, it's actually three comfort foods in one!

> **TIP** *The hot Korean red chile paste called gochujang provides a key flavor for the dish. You can, of course, substitute another red chile paste, but it won't taste quite the same. Luckily, these days you can easily order both gochujang and kimchee online if you can't find them in your local markets. But I strongly recommend that you make your own kimchee using the recipe on page 193.*

FOR THE **STEAK**

- ⅓ cup (70 ml) mirin
- ¼ cup (30 g) grated apple
- 2 tablespoons soy sauce
- 2 tablespoons sliced scallion, white part only
- 1 tablespoon gochujang (Korean red chile paste; see page 21)
- 1 tablespoon minced garlic
- 1 tablespoon grated peeled fresh ginger
- 2 teaspoons sesame oil
- 2 teaspoons rice wine vinegar
- 2 teaspoons honey or brown sugar
- 1½ to 2 pounds (680 to 910 g) skirt steak

FOR THE **KIMCHEE RICE**

- 2 cups (410 g) uncooked sushi rice
- 1 teaspoon kosher salt
- 3 tablespoons canola oil
- 1¾ cups (490 g) kimchee (page 193), cut into bite-size pieces
- 2 tablespoons rice wine vinegar
- 2 teaspoons sugar
- 4 large eggs
- Thinly sliced scallions (optional)

RECIPE FOLLOWS

Make the steak: The day before you want to serve the dish, choose a large zip-top freezer bag or glass baking dish just large enough to hold the steak so the marinade covers it completely. Combine the mirin, apple, soy sauce, scallion, gochujang, garlic, ginger, sesame oil, vinegar, and honey. Cut the steak into even portions, add it to the marinade, then cover or seal and marinate the meat, refrigerated, overnight.

Make the sushi rice: For best results, make it a day or two ahead. If you're not using a rice cooker, as I now do, rinse the rice and place it in a 2-quart (2-L) saucepan with 1½ cups (360 g) water and the salt. (If your hand is resting on top of the rice, the water should just cover your fingers. This is my grandmother's trick, which I have passed on to all of my cooks.)

Cover the pot tightly and bring the water to a boil. Turn the heat to as low as you can go without it being off, and cook for 18 minutes without lifting the lid. After 18 minutes, turn the heat to high for 1 minute without lifting the lid, then turn off the heat and let the pot sit covered for 5 more minutes. Remove the lid, fluff the rice, and set it aside or refrigerate until you make the steak and eggs. (You should have about 4 cups/800 g.)

Make the kimchee rice: In a medium sauté pan over medium heat, warm 2 tablespoons of the canola oil. Add the kimchee, vinegar, and sugar and cook until the kimchee is heated through and softens slightly, about 3 minutes. Fold in the cooked rice and set aside while you cook the steak.

Cook the steak: Heat a grill to medium-high heat or preheat the broiler. The cooking time will vary depending on the thickness of the steak and your preference for doneness. My ideal is to cook it for a few minutes on each side, just until the outside of the steak is slightly charred but the inside is still pink. Drain off the marinade and set the steak pieces on the hot grill or on a broiler pan. Once it's done to your liking, let the steak rest for 10 minutes, then cut it into thin slices on the diagonal against the grain.

Meanwhile, in a large skillet, heat the remaining 1 tablespoon canola oil over medium heat and fry the eggs sunny side up. When they're done, place a large scoop of kimchee rice on each plate, then top them with an equal number of steak slices per plate and one of the eggs. Garnish with sliced scallions, if using.

ROAST CHICKEN

WITH *Chinese black bean sauce*

SERVES 4

When I created this recipe for the opening menu of The Good Fork, I wanted a classic neighborhood bistro roast chicken with some kind of a twist. When I worked for Anita Lo at her restaurant Annisa in Manhattan, she used to make this simple pan sauce with Chinese fermented black beans, vinegar, and wine. It's a great sauce, and the funky flavor of the beans really shines through. But for my dish, I wanted a real chicken gravy—thick and creamy and comforting. So I take that black bean sauce and add a bunch of soft roasted garlic and just puree it. The smell of these beans is a little off-putting owing to their fermentation—much like fish sauce—but when used correctly, those little beans give the dish—I hate to say it—big umami. Most people can't even tell what the gravy's secret ingredient is; they just know something unusual is making it delicious. Serving it with potato-parsnip mash bolstered with cream and butter, as I do, also keeps the classic comfort food level high, but you could also try serving it with a side of braised leeks, sweet cipollini onions, or grilled scallions.

> **TIP** *You should be able to find Shaoxing cooking wine and fermented black beans at nearly any Asian food market and occasionally at larger supermarkets.*

FOR THE **BLACK BEAN SAUCE**

1	tablespoon canola oil
1	shallot, thinly sliced
1	cup (240 ml) white wine
3/4	cup (180 ml) Shaoxing cooking wine
6	cups (1.4 L) chicken stock, or to taste
15	cloves garlic
10	Chinese fermented black beans

FOR THE **ROAST CHICKEN**

4	skin-on chicken breasts
1	tablespoon canola oil
	Kosher salt and freshly ground black pepper
3	tablespoons cold unsalted butter, cut into 3 pieces

RECIPE FOLLOWS

Make the sauce: In a large saucepan or Dutch oven, heat the canola oil over low heat and cook the shallot until it softens and becomes translucent. Add both wines and reduce the liquid until you have about ¾ (180 ml) cup.

Add the stock, garlic, and black beans and bring it to a boil. Turn the heat to low and reduce the liquid to about 2 cups (480 ml). Strain out the solids, saving the garlic and discarding the rest.

Place the garlic cloves and the liquid in a blender and puree until it is smooth. Set aside. This sauce can be made ahead and refrigerated for 2 to 3 days or even frozen.

Make the chicken: Preheat the oven to 450°F (230°C). Pat the chicken breasts dry and season the skin side only liberally with salt.

Set a cast-iron or ovenproof pan large enough to hold all four breasts comfortably over medium-high heat. Do not use nonstick; you want to encourage the brown bits that form on the bottom of the pan. Add the oil and swirl it so that it fully coats the pan. When the oil just begins to smoke, add the chicken breasts skin side down, making sure not to crowd them.

Cook the chicken without turning it over until the skin turns light golden brown, turning down the heat if the skin begins to darken too quickly. Season the flesh side of the chicken with salt and pepper, flip the breasts skin side up, and put the pan in the oven for 12 to 15 minutes, until the skin is deep golden-brown.

When the chicken is done, remove it to a platter to rest and return the hot pan to the stove over medium-high heat. Add 1 cup (240 ml) of the black bean sauce and bring it to a low boil, scraping off the browned bits on the bottom of the pan as the sauce heats through.

Taste the sauce: If it is too salty, add a little water or chicken stock to taste. Reduce the heat to low, swirl in the cold butter, and whisk it in to emulsify the sauce.

To serve, top each breast with sauce and serve immediately.

SOY-BRAISED SHORT RIBS

SERVES 6

This recipe is the grown-up version of the classic Korean short-rib dish called *kalbi jim*. Koreans generally don't consume a lot of meat, despite the proliferation of barbecue restaurants in the United States. Our diets are really based around plant life, seafood, and seaweed. So this is a special-occasion feast dish, both there and here. In fact, when my mom made it back in Korea, I would always wonder who was getting married! It's also a winter dish. You cook it slowly and you stay warm all day. Koreans usually just boil the meat, but I like to apply some French technique and braise it in red wine for a little roundness and skim off the extra fat before I finish it. At the restaurant I serve it with black rice and garnish it with kimchee, ribbons of thinly sliced fried beaten eggs, scallions, crushed chestnuts, and sesame seeds, but just one or two of those is all you need. At home, I like to serve this with black rice and, of course, lots of kimchee.

> **TIP** *Like any braise, this is best if left to sit for a day so that the flavors meld. In that case, refrigerate the ribs and sauce separately, and skip skimming the fat from the sauce until you remove it from the refrigerator the next day.*

	Canola or grapeseed oil for sautéing
4	to 5 pounds (1.8 to 2.3 kg) bone-in beef short ribs, about 5 inches (12 cm) long
	Kosher salt and freshly ground black pepper
1	large onion, cut into large dice
3	cloves garlic, crushed
1/3	cup (35 g) peeled fresh ginger chunks
2	cups (480 ml) red wine
2	cups (480 ml) water or chicken stock
3/4	cup (180 ml) soy sauce
1/2	packed cup (110 g) brown sugar
1/2	cup (120 ml) mirin
1	cup (280 g) diced kimchee (page 193) or Korean pickled daikon

Crushed chestnuts, toasted sesame seeds, sliced scallions, and slivers of fried beaten eggs, for garnish (optional)

Add just enough canola oil to coat the bottom of a wide, heavy-bottomed pot with straight sides and heat it over high heat. Season the ribs lightly with salt and pepper and sear them well on all sides. Remove the ribs and set them aside.

In the same pot, add enough canola oil to cover the bottom, if needed, and sauté the onion, garlic, and 1 chunk of ginger for 5 minutes over medium-high heat, or until they begin to soften, then add the wine and let it reduce by half.

Add the water, soy sauce, brown sugar, and mirin and bring them to a boil, then add half of the kimchee, 1 teaspoon salt, and 1/4 teaspoon pepper.

Return the ribs to the pan. The liquid should come at least three quarters of the way up the sides of the ribs. If not, add more water or chicken stock.

Reduce the heat to low and simmer slowly for 2½ hours, covered. Check after 2 hours; if the meat is falling off the bone but not falling apart, the ribs are ready. Remove the ribs from the pan.

Strain the sauce. Skim off and discard as much fat as you can with a ladle. Serve the ribs covered with the sauce and garnished with the remaining ½ cup (140 g) chopped kimchee and, if you like, with one or more of the optional toppings. Serve cooked rice on the side.

GRILLED MARINATED SHRIMP

WITH *vegetable risotto*

SERVES 4 TO 6

This was my very first summer risotto dish, and my goal was to keep it simple to showcase how good a well-made risotto can be. Risotto is on a lot of menus, but most restaurants will fail you; it will be either undercooked and crunchy or overcooked and too mushy. People are usually put off by the stirring—that whole idea of a *nonna* standing hunched over the pot for hours. But it really only takes half an hour, and you can even walk away for a minute or two, though neglect will make this into cooked rice rather than risotto. The stirring—the agitation—is the key to making it creamy. It's also important to have your hot stock ready to go when you begin making the dish.

FOR THE SHRIMP

2	pounds (910 g) large tail-on shrimp, cleaned and deveined
1	lemon, zested and juiced (reserve the peel)
4	small sprigs fresh thyme, plus extra leaves for garnish (optional)
2	tablespoons extra-virgin olive oil
	Freshly ground black pepper

FOR THE RISOTTO

6	cups (1.4 L) chicken stock
1/4	cup (60 ml) plus 1 tablespoon extra-virgin olive oil
1	cup (190 g) 1/2-inch (12-mm) cubes zucchini
1	large onion, finely diced
2	tablespoons minced garlic
2	cups (400 g) Arborio rice
1	cup (240 ml) good-quality white wine
6	tablespoons (3/4 stick/85 g) cold unsalted butter
1/3	cup (30 g) grated Parmigiano-Reggiano cheese
1	cup (135 g) cherry tomatoes, sliced in half
1	cup (100 g) sugar snap peas, sliced diagonally into 1/4-inch (6-mm) strips
	Kosher salt and freshly ground black pepper
1	scallion, green part only, thinly sliced for garnish

Make the shrimp: In a large bowl or container, combine the shrimp, the lemon zest and juice, thyme, and olive oil. Cut the zested lemon peel into quarters and add it to the bowl, then season the mixture well with pepper. Toss to coat the shrimp and let them marinate in the refrigerator for at least 30 minutes or up to 2 hours.

Make the risotto: In a medium pot, bring the chicken stock and 3 cups (720 ml) water to a boil, then turn down the heat to keep it at a very low simmer.

In a large pot, heat 1 tablespoon of the olive oil over medium-high heat. Add the zucchini and cook, turning occasionally, until it's nicely browned, about 5 minutes. Remove the zucchini from the pan and set aside.

Turn the heat to medium and add the remaining ¼ cup (60 ml) of the olive oil. Add the onion and cook, stirring frequently so that it begins to soften but doesn't brown, about 4 minutes. Add the garlic and cook for 3 more minutes, or until the onion is translucent and the garlic is soft. Add the rice, turn the heat to medium-high and cook until the rice smells toasted and sticks to the pot, about 3 minutes.

Add the wine and stir with a wooden spoon or spatula, scraping up the bits from the bottom of the pan. Cook, stirring continuously, until the wine has evaporated.

Slowly pour in enough stock to completely cover the rice. Stir almost constantly until the rice absorbs the stock. Add another ladleful of stock and stir until it is absorbed, and repeat until you've used all the stock and the rice is cooked to al dente—or with a bit of chew left in the middle of each grain—about 20 minutes.

Remove the pan from the heat and vigorously stir in the butter. Stir in the cheese, cooked zucchini, tomatoes, and snap peas until they are warmed through. Season with salt and pepper and cover while you cook the shrimp.

Working as quickly as you can so the risotto stays warm, heat a grill or skillet over medium-high heat. Remove the shrimp from the marinade and grill or cook them until pink and firm, about 2 minutes per side.

To serve, top the risotto with a few shrimp and garnish with the scallions and the thyme leaves, if using.

"GREEN EGGS AND HAM" RISOTTO

SERVES 4 TO 6

When the kids were little and I was reading Dr. Seuss to them a lot—and I wanted risotto for dinner—I dreamed up this green bowl laced with slivers of ham and topped with an egg yolk for the restaurant. If you can't easily find quail eggs, I'd recommend you omit the egg yolks altogether, as regular chicken yolks are just too big and will overpower the risotto. At the restaurant, I used to top this dish with pan-seared scallops, which turns this dish into a full and elegant meal for a dinner party.

FOR THE GREEN PUREE

½ cup (65 g) thawed frozen peas
½ cup (80 g) thawed frozen spinach
½ cup (25 g) fresh flat-leaf parsley leaves

FOR THE RISOTTO

4 ounces (115 g) thinly sliced Serrano ham
Canola or grapeseed oil, for frying
6 cups (1.4 L) chicken stock
¼ cup (60 ml) extra-virgin olive oil
1 large onion, finely diced
2 tablespoons minced garlic
2 cups (400 g) Arborio rice
1 cup (240 ml) good-quality dry white wine
6 tablespoons (¾ stick/85 g) cold unsalted butter
1 cup (135 g) frozen peas
⅓ cup (30 g) grated Parmigiano-Reggiano cheese
1 teaspoon kosher salt
Chopped fresh chives, for garnish
1 lemon, cut into wedges
4 to 6 quail eggs

Make the green puree: In a food processor, combine the peas, spinach, and parsley. Puree until smooth, adding up to ½ cup (120 ml) water if needed. Set aside.

Make the risotto: Cut the ham lengthwise into ½-inch (12-mm) strips. In a cast-iron skillet, heat 1 inch (2.5 cm) canola oil over medium-high heat until it shimmers. Making sure the strips are separated, deep-fry the ham for about 30 seconds, until curly and crisp, working in batches if necessary so that you don't crowd the pan. Drain on paper towels.

In a medium pot, bring the chicken stock and 3 cups (720 ml) water to a boil, then turn down the heat to keep it at a very low simmer.

In a large pot, heat the olive oil over medium-high heat. Add the onion and cook, stirring frequently so that it begins to soften but doesn't brown, about 4 minutes. Add the garlic and cook for 3 minutes more, or until the onion is translucent and the garlic is soft. Add the rice, turn the heat to medium-high, and cook until the rice smells toasted and sticks to the pot, about 3 minutes. Add the wine and stir with a wooden spoon or spatula, scraping up the bits from the bottom of the pan. Cook, stirring continuously, until the wine has evaporated.

Slowly pour in enough stock to completely cover the rice. Stir almost constantly until the rice absorbs the stock. Add another ladleful of stock and stir until it is absorbed, and repeat until you've used all the stock and the rice is cooked to al dente—or with a bit of chew left in the middle of each grain—about 20 minutes.

Remove the pan from the heat and vigorously stir in the butter. Stir in the green puree, frozen peas, cheese, and salt.

Put a portion of risotto in each dish and top with fried ham, chives, and a squeeze of fresh lemon juice. Make a small indentation in the top of each risotto portion. Working over a sink or bowl, crack open one quail egg into the palm of your hand and let most of the white drip through your fingers. Nestle one yolk in the indentation on the top of each dish. Serve immediately.

BUTTERMILK PANNA COTTA

WITH *seasonal berries*

SERVES 6

When I first wrote our opening menu for the restaurant, Ben pointed out to me that I hadn't included any desserts! The desserts that I do love tend to be classic: chocolate cake, carrot cake, and something like this—it's smooth, creamy, and only a slightly sweet end to a meal. You can use whatever berries you like or that are in season: blueberries, raspberries, strawberries, or a mix of a few. My little pet peeve about panna cotta is that you shouldn't use too much powdered gelatin, because it will end up too gelatinous. *Smooth* is the operative word! Note that while it only takes twenty minutes to prepare, you'll need to factor in another four hours of chilling time.

FOR THE PANNA COTTA

2	tablespoons cold water
1 1/4	teaspoons powdered unflavored gelatin
1/2	cup (120 ml) heavy cream
1/3	cup (65 g) sugar
1	vanilla bean
	Pinch of salt
2	cups (480 ml) buttermilk

FOR THE FRUIT TOPPING

1	pint (340 g) fresh berries
1	tablespoon sugar
2	teaspoons fresh lemon juice

Make the panna cotta: Put the water in a small bowl and sprinkle the gelatin over it evenly; set aside to let it "bloom."

In a small saucepan, whisk together the cream and sugar. Split the vanilla bean, scrape the seeds into the pan, and then add the pod and the salt. Bring the cream to a low boil over medium heat, stirring occasionally and watching to make sure the cream doesn't boil over. As soon it reaches a low boil, remove it from the heat and transfer the contents of the saucepan to a large bowl.

Whisk about one third of the buttermilk into the hot cream, so the mixture is warm but not hot. Whisk in the bloomed gelatin and then the remainder of the buttermilk.

Strain the mixture into a pitcher, discarding the vanilla bean pod. Pour the custard into six 4-ounce (60-ml) ramekins or small serving glasses, wrap loosely with plastic wrap, and refrigerate them for at least 4 hours.

Meanwhile, make the fruit topping: Wash the berries and trim the stems or blemished spots if necessary. In a medium bowl, toss the fruit with the sugar and lemon juice. Let it sit for at least 20 minutes until ready to use, storing the bowl in the refrigerator. If the fruit will rest longer than 1 hour, bring it to room temperature before you serve the dish.

When the panna cotta is firm, serve each ramekin topped with the macerated berries.

CHOCOLATE BREAD PUDDING

SERVES 8 TO 10

This is one of my all-time favorite Good Fork desserts, because it's got chocolate. You should make this recipe when you have extra bread kicking around. It's best with brioche, but it can be quite yummy with other leftover loaves, such as ciabatta or even a mix of different breads.

1   cup (145 g) raisins

3   tablespoons rum

8   cups (280 g) 1-inch (2.5-cm) cubes brioche, crusts removed

½   cup (1 stick/115 g) unsalted butter, melted

6   ounces (175 g) bittersweet chocolate, or 1 cup (175 g) semisweet chocolate chips

3   cups (720 ml) heavy cream

1   cup (240 ml) milk

1   cup (200 g) sugar

6   large eggs

½   teaspoon vanilla extract

Pinch of salt

Whipped cream or ice cream, for serving (optional)

In a small bowl, soak the raisins in the rum; set aside.

Line a medium baking pan with foil. Put the cubed bread on it, then drizzle it with the melted butter.

Break the chocolate into small pieces if needed and set them aside in a large heatproof bowl. In a large heavy-bottomed pan, mix together the cream, milk, and sugar. Warm the mixture over medium-high heat, stirring occasionally, until it begins to steam and release an air bubble or two—not quite a boil. Pour the hot cream mixture over the chocolate, then whisk the chocolate into the cream.

In another large bowl, beat the eggs. Whisk the warm cream mixture into the beaten eggs, 1 cup (240 ml) at a time. This will be your custard. Stir in the vanilla and salt.

Sprinkle the soaked raisins over the bread, then mix any remaining rum into the custard. Pour the custard over the bread cubes, making sure each piece is submerged. Cover and soak it, refrigerated, for at least 1 hour or up to overnight.

To bake, preheat the oven to 325°F (165°C). Remove the pudding from the refrigerator and cover it loosely with foil. Bake for 30 minutes, then uncover and bake 15 minutes more, or until the pudding is set but still a little wobbly.

Let it cool for about 1 hour, then serve slices warm, topped with whipped cream or ice cream if desired.

ESSAY

BUILDING THE GOOD FORK

Those who know me know I'm always looking for a new project—something to build or create. Even as a kid, I had a workbench and woodworking tools in my room in my parents' Upper West Side apartment. Carpentry and building are what I did to make some money through college, where I studied theater, and as I pursued an acting career in Chicago, D.C., and New York in the years before Sohui and I opened The Good Fork.

I learned a bit from my dad early on, and later I was fortunate to learn under some woodworkers who were true artists. But I was both inspired and schooled by a community in Vermont that my uncle moved his family to in the 1970s. It was founded by a group of architects, mostly out of Yale University, who started an experimental community, building land and building houses. It wasn't a commune, but they were kind of hippies—very adventurous and full of new ideas. It's one of the reasons we live in Red Hook now; it reminded me of that sort of community, with a small-town sort of vibe. My uncle's group built all plywood and Plexiglas structures and they'd throw crazy parties—every year, we would build a float for the Fourth of July, and we still do.

The way those guys would build their floats really made an impression on me as a youngster—their ability to create these incredible structures so quickly, really designing as they went, rather than working from a plan. One of the things that I learned from them was the approach called "design/build"—that the builder is also the designer, and you create the design as you go. You have an idea of what you want to build, and you know where you're headed, but as you go, you change your course based on how things are looking, what you have on hand, and how materials are behaving. It's a lot like cooking, in fact, and that's pretty much how I built the restaurant.

A restaurant needs a strong sense of place and a sense of adventure if it's going to help you leave your troubles behind. There's this famous bar in London called Gordon's Wine Bar. It's halfway underground, down a staircase, and has vaulted stone ceilings that somehow make the space seem cozy instead of cramped. When you have a low ceiling, if it's a sharp edge it feels depressing, but when you curve the ceiling into the wall, it feels cozy. When you're in there drinking, it's so easy to be only there. That was my inspiration for how to make the most of a space that was essentially going to be a little box of a deli when we bought it. Then I just carried that theme through: I like clean lines but those that are soft; I think the gentle curve is a really pretty thing to the eye. I was thinking about dining cars in old trains, and the riveted fuselage of an airplane. I used a mix of amber wood and metal, and I added twinkling lights to the trees in the backyard, plus an enclosed patio that feels as much like a sunporch as a second dining room.

People now compare our front dining room to the hull of a ship, and they're not far off. It has a tiny bar with a few stools, beyond which you can peek into the galley kitchen that's built to fit Sohui's small frame. The tables are made from wood from a barn up in Vermont on my family's property, the entryway is a glass door from an old tuxedo shop that I got at a thrift store in Chicago years ago, and the wood around it was picked from framing timbers in the neighborhood. I built it all with the help of a couple of friends.

A restaurant is like a boat: Every inch matters. You've got equipment, codes, and the comfort of guests to think about, plus the flow of servers moving around each other as efficiently as possible in a small space. Miss the mark, and you're uncomfortable, on top of each other, and eventually closed for business. Pull it off well, and your environment becomes part of the romance of the restaurant.

That actually was the easy part. I also had to learn how to create a beverage program, pair wine, make espresso, manage the front of the house, and wait tables—something I surprisingly never did throughout my thirty years of acting.

BEN SCHNEIDER, 2016

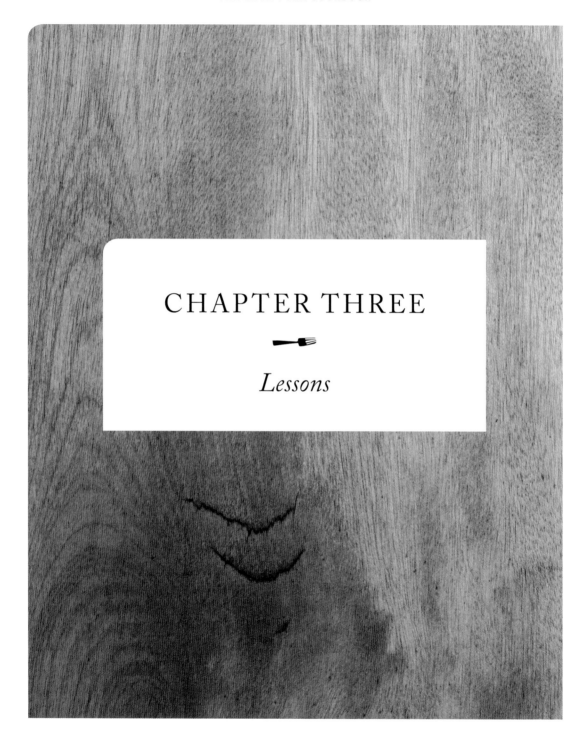

CHAPTER THREE

Lessons

WHEN I WAS PREGNANT WITH MY DAUGHTER, JASPER, I naively figured I'd be back to work full-time after she was born. I had lined up my friend Sawako Okochi, a very talented cook, to help me for six months, but I had no idea how intense it would be to have a baby. Sawa ended up staying for four years—through the birth of my son, Oliver, too. Sawa was my proxy: We worked together on the menu and specials like quinoa-stuffed squid or apple-braised pork with white bean ragout each day, but she filled in for me during service so I didn't have to be there every night until midnight working the line. In fact, Ben and I used to joke that we both had doppelgängers when we weren't in the restaurant. Sawa, who is Japanese, was me, and then my old Annisa colleague and friend, Aaron Petrovich, a bearded white guy like Ben, helped manage the dining room.

When I was pregnant with Oliver and still doing all the daytime prep work, my doctor finally insisted I stop standing in a hot kitchen all day, my belly right up against the stove. So I hired Rigo Vazquez to help Sawa. A Mexican immigrant, Rigo had been the head cook at Florent, a famous late-night bistro in the Meatpacking District, which closed in 2008. Over the years, I have developed a familial friendship with Rigo. Working together, we have bonded over our immigrant past; our children, who are the same age; and our passion to make delicious food. I taught him how to make my kimchee, dumplings, and Korean steak marinades. But I realized Rigo knew what it took to be creative and to put a dish together. So I started teaching him sauces, braises, and how a restaurant like ours builds flavor from scratch. (He also influenced many of our dishes over time, and brought us lots of knowledge of chiles and the amazing Flan-Impossible Cake on page 140.)

This period of The Good Fork taught me a lot, and not just about how to balance work and parenting. I originally thought I could just put people in management positions and walk away, but I found out a mom-and-pop restaurant like ours needs constant attention from the mother and father, because so much of it is our personality. I also learned how to be a good boss, working with my cooks to help them develop the confidence to do whatever it was they wanted to do next: for Sawa, to eventually open her own restaurant, called Shalom Japan; for Rigo, to grow into a true chef.

FRIED OYSTER PO' BOYS

WITH *rémoulade* AND *pickled red onions*

SERVES 4

For my fortieth birthday, I took a weekend trip to New Orleans with my favorite gal pals. I was always a little obsessed with the food there. I love everything gooey, stewy, and fried. This oyster po' boy was a result of that trip. It is important not to overcook the oysters, because you want their soft, creamy interiors as a counterpoint to the fried exterior. If you buy the largest, meatiest oysters you can find, that helps; small ones won't provide as much satisfactory contrast. At the restaurant, I prefer to make these on little brioche rolls baked by a French bakery and serve them as a trio, but at home, purchased potato rolls from Martin's Famous Pastry Shoppe are just as good. It might not be a totally traditional approach, but to my credit, Alan Richman—*GQ*'s famous food writer—loved these.

| **TIP** *For the best flavor, make the pickled onions at least a day and up to 48 hours before making the po' boys. The rémoulade can also be made a day or two in advance.*

FOR THE PICKLED RED ONIONS

- ½ cup (120 ml) red wine vinegar
- ¼ cup (60 ml) cold water
- 3 tablespoons sugar
- 2 tablespoons salt
- 1 medium red onion, thinly sliced from root to stem

FOR THE RÉMOULADE

- ¼ cup (60 ml) sour cream
- ¼ cup (60 ml) mayonnaise
- 2 tablespoons whole-grain mustard
- 2 tablespoons chopped dill pickles
  Generous pinch cayenne pepper
- ¼ teaspoon paprika
  Freshly ground black pepper

FOR THE PO' BOYS

- 3 cups (720 ml) vegetable or another neutral oil
- 2 pounds (910 g) shucked oysters
- ¾ cup (135 g) fine cornmeal
- 4 potato rolls or buns, toasted
- 1 handful baby arugula, washed and dried

Make the pickled red onions: In a nonreactive container large enough to hold the onion, combinine the vinegar, cold water, sugar, and salt. Whisk to dissolve the sugar, then add the onion; cover and refrigerate for several hours and up to 2 days before you make the po' boys.

Make the rémoulade: In a small mixing bowl, whisk to combine the sour cream, mayonnaise, mustard, pickles, cayenne, paprika, and black pepper to taste. Set aside, or refrigerate if you won't be making the po' boys immediately.

Make the po' boys: Heat the vegetable oil in a Dutch oven or heavy-bottomed pot until a thermometer registers 350°F (175°C).

Line a baking sheet with paper towels. Drain the oysters, dredge them in the cornmeal, and fry them a few at a time for 1 minute, or until a crispy cornmeal crust develops, then drain them on the paper towels.

Assemble the po' boys by spreading 2 teaspoons rémoulade on either side of each roll. Layer each with red onions, a few oysters, and some arugula leaves. Serve immediately.

SPRING PEA CROQUETTES

WITH *fennel jam*

MAKES ABOUT 15 CROQUETTES; SERVES 4 TO 6

This idea came from a trip to an Indian restaurant where the *samosa* was terrible—like lead. I wanted to make my own version that had those great flavors but wasn't so heavy. Increasing the quantity of peas made the filling lighter, and then I got rid of the dough completely, so it basically became a croquette breaded in panko. Toasting the spices whole before you grind them really brings out their fragrance, and ground spices don't last as long as people think they do. There's a world of difference when you toast and grind from whole, so take the extra time to do it. I'm a big fan of savory jams. When you cook anything down and concentrate its flavor, it becomes really sweet, but not cloying. It makes a great condiment for grilled meats and crostini, as well. At the restaurant, we also serve these croquettes with homemade yogurt seasoned with salt and pepper and a little lemon zest. We make our own yogurt (see page 157) and strain it. You can buy thicker Middle Eastern *labne*, strained plain yogurt, or start all the way from scratch, as we do.

> TIP *The potatoes can be leftover mashed potatoes from the night before, or you can simply boil and smash a couple of russets.*

FOR THE FENNEL JAM

2	tablespoons olive oil
1	medium onion, diced
4	cups (400 g) diced fennel bulb
1	tablespoon sugar
2	tablespoons fennel seeds
1/2	cup (120 ml) Pernod Anise liqueur
	Cayenne pepper
	Kosher salt and freshly ground black pepper

FOR THE CROQUETTES

1 1/2	tablespoons coriander seeds
1 1/2	teaspoons cumin seeds
3/4	teaspoon fennel seeds
2	teaspoons canola oil, plus more for frying
1	medium onion, finely diced
1 1/2	tablespoons minced peeled fresh ginger
1/2	red Holland or Anaheim chile, seeded and minced
1 1/2	teaspoons garam masala
2	cups (270 g) frozen peas, thawed, or fresh spring peas
2	cups (420 g) mashed potatoes
3	cups (160 g) panko
	Kosher salt

Make the fennel jam: In your biggest skillet, heat the olive oil over medium heat. Sauté the onion and fennel bulb with the sugar and fennel seeds until the mixture caramelizes and becomes a deep, nutty brown.

Add the Pernod, then stir until any browned bits are loosened from the bottom of the pan. Remove the pan from the heat.

Use a blender to puree half of the onion-fennel mixture, then add it back to the pan. Stir to mix well and season with cayenne, salt, and black pepper. Set aside.

Make the croquettes: Heat a dry skillet over medium-high heat, then toast the coriander, cumin, and fennel seeds; shake them around in the hot pan until they smell fragrant and toasty. Grind them in a spice grinder (a clean coffee grinder also works well) and set aside.

Add the canola oil to the pan and return the pan to medium heat. Sweat the onion, ginger, and chile until translucent and a little browned around the edges, about 10 minutes. Stir in the toasted spices and garam masala, and cook for just a minute longer.

Transfer the onion-spice mixture to a large bowl. In a blender or food processor, puree half of this mixture, then return it to the bowl. Fold in the peas, mashed potatoes, and 2 cups (105 g) of the panko. Season with salt to taste. This is your croquette dough. If it is too soft to work with, refrigerate it until it is firm but pliable.

To prepare the croquettes, heat 2 inches (5 cm) of canola oil in a deep, heavy-bottomed pot or Dutch oven over medium heat to 350°F (175°C).

Meanwhile, shape the dough into golf ball–sized pieces and place them on a baking sheet. Line another baking sheet with a few layers of paper towels, and put the remaining 1 cup (55 g) panko in a bowl.

When you are ready to fry the croquettes, roll each croquette in the panko and then drop it into the hot oil. Fry them just a few at a time, until they are a deep golden brown, 2 to 3 minutes, then set them aside to drain on the paper towels.

When all of the croquettes are fried, serve them hot with the fennel jam.

THE GOOD FORK BURGER

WITH *bacon jam* AND *tempura sweet onion rings*

SERVES 4

In good restaurants, a burger is often what I order when I can't make up my mind, because it never disappoints. Even so, I didn't want to put one on my own menu. It was another fight Ben eventually won. This is a neighborhood joint in a laid-back neighborhood, he reasoned with me—we gotta put a burger on. And burger bloggers, of which there are many in New York City, also proved him right with their positive reviews. The late Josh Ozersky, one of the country's best-known food writers and a burger aficionado, loved this burger. In my opinion, the key to a really great burger is that it must be seasoned well with salt, or no addition of mayo, mustard, and ketchup will really help. I also want to encourage you to skip the bacon jam to keep things simple or go with other toppings. In fact, I, along with our cooks, prefer a burger topped with bacon, kimchee, and blue cheese. You'd think that combination would be really horrible, but it's amazing—you can order it that way at The Good Fork, too.

TIP *If you're in a rush, just pick up a packet of ground beef, mix it with salt, and grill it, but if you are so inclined, ask your butcher to freshly grind a mixture of sirloin and chuck or sirloin and short ribs. The difference is remarkable! And for goodness' sake, don't play with the burger by pressing it with the spatula as it cooks.*

FOR THE BACON JAM

5	strips bacon, roughly chopped
4	cups (500 grams) minced onions
¼	cup (60 ml) balsamic vinegar
	Pinch crushed red pepper flakes
1	tablespoon brown sugar
	Kosher salt and freshly ground black pepper

FOR THE BURGERS

2	pounds (910 g) ground beef (see Tip)
1	tablespoon plus 1 teaspoon salt
4	hamburger buns, grilled or toasted
4	leaves Boston, romaine, or another hearty lettuce
4	tomato slices
4	to 8 red onion slices
	Dill pickles for garnish
	Tempura Sweet Onion Rings (recipe follows)

RECIPE FOLLOWS

Make the bacon jam: In a skillet over medium-low heat, cook the bacon until almost crisp and the fat is rendered, about 10 minutes.

Remove the bacon from the pan, setting it aside, and cook the onions in the fat over very low heat, until they are caramelized.

Return the bacon to the pan along with the vinegar, chile flakes, and brown sugar. Cook over low heat for 30 minutes, stirring occasionally, then season with salt and pepper and set aside while you make the burgers and onion rings. You can make this in advance, but bring it to room temperature before you serve it. It will last for up to 2 weeks in the refrigerator.

Make the burgers: Shape the ground beef into four patties on waxed paper set into a baking sheet, being careful not to overwork the meat because it toughens it. Make a big indent in the middle of each burger with two fingers—so that you could rest a golf ball in

the hole—which will prevent the patty from becoming a meatball rather than a patty when cooked. Liberally season the patties with the salt and place them in the refrigerator until you are ready to cook them. (If you are making the onion rings, start them now.)

Heat a gas or charcoal grill to high heat—you should only be able to hold your hand over the flame for a few seconds—then oil the grate and cook the burgers until they are done to your liking, 3 to 4 minutes per side for medium-rare. (You can also cook them on a skillet over high heat with a tiny amount of olive oil or other fat.) Remove the burgers to a plate and let them rest for at least 10 minutes, or keep them warm tented with foil while you fry the onion rings.

To assemble the burgers, spread the bacon jam on the buns, top with the patties, lettuce, tomato, and red onion slices, and serve with pickles and a pile of hot onion rings.

TEMPURA SWEET ONION RINGS

SERVES 4

I also like to think my burger works so well because I served it not with French fries but onion rings, with a recipe I really slaved over. In fact, at first I so rarely trusted my cooks to make them perfectly, I often made them myself. One of the tricks is softening the sharpness of the onion in a buttermilk bath, and the other is the batter. It's just the right thickness, and it's also applied right before the onions go into the fryer. That's important.

2	large Vidalia or sweet onions, cut into ½-inch (12-mm) rounds
1	cup (240 ml) buttermilk
	Vegetable oil, for frying
½	cup (65 g) all-purpose flour
¼	cup (30 g) cornstarch
½	teaspoon kosher salt
¾	cup (180 ml) cold seltzer water

Separate the rings of the onions and soak them in the buttermilk for about 30 minutes at room temperature. Meanwhile, line a baking sheet or tray with paper towels and heat 3 inches (7.5 cm) of oil in a deep-sided, heavy-bottomed pot to 350°F (175°C)—the oil should be shimmering but not smoking.

In a large bowl, whisk together the flour, cornstarch, and salt, then quickly whisk in the cold seltzer. Some lumps are okay—the texture should be like a light pancake batter. Test the temperature of the oil by dropping in a little batter; it should sizzle and bubble up right away without burning.

Dip 2 or 3 rings into the batter and then immediately drop them into the hot oil. Cook them until golden brown, about 2 minutes per side, and then drain them on the paper towels. Repeat these steps, working in small batches.

APPLE-BRAISED BERKSHIRE PORK SHOULDER

WITH *navy bean ragout, mustard greens,* AND *guanciale crumble*

SERVES 8 TO 10

This was one of many dishes that I created in the pursuit of using more affordable cuts of meat, which is just as helpful at a restaurant on a budget as in a home kitchen. I originally used oxtails in my Good Fork braises, which cook up awesomely rich, but pork shoulder is easier to come by. I do prefer to use Berkshire pork shoulder, which is a heritage or older breed that is becoming easier to find and has a little more fat and connective tissue, turning the dish into a slow-cooked, succulent, subtle comforting dish. You can really use any pork shoulder, but Berkshire or another fatty breed of pork will give you the best results. Don't skip the crumble—it's easy to put together and it provides a satisfying contrasting texture to a dish that is otherwise several layers of softness.

> TIP *You can make all of these components in advance.*

FOR THE BEANS

- 1 pound (455 g) dry navy beans
- 1 medium onion, cut into medium dice
- 3 medium carrots, cut into medium dice
- 5 cloves garlic, minced
- 1 bay leaf
- 1 small bunch mustard greens, stems removed and roughly chopped
  Kosher salt and freshly ground black pepper
  Juice of 1 lemon (about 3 tablespoons)

FOR THE BRAISE

- 1 cup (125 g) all-purpose flour
- 2 teaspoons kosher salt
  Freshly ground black pepper
- 1 boneless Berkshire pork shoulder (4 pounds/1.8 kg), cut into 2½-inch (6-cm) cubes
  Olive oil
- 1 medium fennel bulb, cut lengthwise into eighths
- 5 cloves garlic, smashed with the side of a knife
- 2 medium carrots, cut into large chunks
- 2 cups (270 g) diced white or yellow onion
- 2 cups (480 ml) white wine
- 3 whole peeled canned tomatoes
- 2 large Medjool dates, pitted
- 1 quart (960 ml) chicken stock
- 2 medium apples, peeled and cut into large chunks
- 3 sprigs fresh thyme
- 1 bay leaf

FOR THE CRUMBLE

- 8 ounces (225 g) guanciale or slab bacon, very finely diced
- ⅔ cup (55 g) panko
- 2 tablespoons minced fresh parsley
- 1 sprig fresh thyme, stems removed

RECIPE FOLLOWS

The night before you want to make this dish, soak the beans: Cover them with several inches of water and a pinch of salt and let them soak overnight.

Make the braise: Preheat the oven to 300°F (150°C).

In a medium bowl, mix the flour with the salt, seasoning to taste with black pepper. Dredge the cubes of pork in the flour mixture, shake off the excess, then set them aside on a plate or baking sheet.

Heat enough olive oil to cover the bottom of a Dutch oven or ovenproof pot over medium heat. Working in batches so as not to crowd the pan, brown the pork on all sides, about 2 minutes per side, and set it aside. (Watch the pan carefully to make sure the flour is not blackening in the pan; if it does, lower the heat.)

Once all the pork has been browned, add the fennel, garlic, carrots, and onion to the pan and sauté them until the onions are translucent, about 5 minutes. Add the wine and increase the heat to high, cooking until the wine begins to boil. Turn down the heat to maintain a steady simmer and reduce the wine by half.

Add the tomatoes and dates, breaking the tomatoes up with your spoon or spatula, then the stock, apples, thyme, and bay leaf. Add the pork once all the ingredients are well incorporated, then cover, transfer to the oven, and cook for 3 hours, turning the meat pieces over about halfway through.

While the pork cooks, make the crumble: In a skillet over medium-high heat, cook the guanciale until it is crispy, about 5 minutes. Strain off most of the fat and reserve it for the beans, then return the pan to the heat and stir in the panko, making sure the fat is well incorporated. Cook until the breadcrumbs are heated through and slightly crispy and brown, about 3 minutes. Add the parsley and thyme, stirring to mix, then turn off the heat and set the crumble aside.

Make the beans: In a Dutch oven or ovenproof pot, heat the reserved bacon fat over medium-high heat. Add the onion, carrots, and garlic, and cook, stirring occasionally, until they are soft and translucent but not brown, about 7 minutes. Add the drained beans, bay leaf, and 6 cups (1.4 L) water. Bring the pot to a boil, then cover it with foil, and place it the oven.

Bake the beans for 45 minutes, then stir in the mustard greens and bake, uncovered, for 30 minutes more, or until the beans are tender and cooked through. Stir them periodically, adding more water if necessary to keep the beans covered. Remove them from the oven and keep warm. Just before serving, season them to taste with salt, pepper, and lemon juice.

Serve the dish in a bowl—either in individual portions or family-style—beans on the bottom, topped by the braise, and then sprinkled with the crumble.

QUICK PASTA

WITH *almond–cherry tomato pesto*

SERVES 6 TO 8

My mother-in-law—who spent a lot of time in Sicily, where she worked as an anthropologist—taught me this very traditional Sicilian pesto pasta dish. The pesto's proper name is *pesto alla Trapanese*, named after Trapani, on Sicily's western coast. It's traditionally served on *busiate*, which is a long, coiled pasta that looks a little like ringlets. I usually make it with Patty Gentry's delicious Sungold cherry tomatoes from Early Girl Farm, but you can substitute ripe slicing tomatoes. It's a quick and easy (and no-cook) sauce that adds up to a fabulous summer dinner for a crowd.

FOR THE **ALMOND–CHERRY TOMATO PESTO**

⅓	cup (35 g) slivered almonds
1	pint (290 g) sweet cherry tomatoes, such as Sungold
½	cup (13 g) loosely packed fresh basil, plus extra for garnish
1	or 2 cloves garlic, sliced
1	teaspoon kosher salt
½	cup (120 ml) extra-virgin olive oil, plus extra for garnish
⅓	cup (30 g) grated Parmigiano-Reggiano or Pecorino-Romano cheese, plus extra for garnish
2	tablespoons unsalted butter

FOR THE **PASTA**

1	pound (455 g) dried pasta

Make the pesto: Preheat the oven to 300°F (150°C). Put the almonds in a dry ovenproof pan and toast them for 10 to 15 minutes, shaking the pan once or twice, until they are very lightly browned and smell nutty. Set them aside to cool.

Place the cherry tomatoes, basil, garlic, and salt in the jar of a blender. Blend, slowly drizzling in the olive oil, until the mixture is smooth. Transfer the pesto to a large serving bowl and fold in the cheese. Season with salt and pepper and add the butter to the bowl.

Meanwhile, make the pasta: Cook it in boiling water to al dente and drain it, saving 1 cup (240 ml) of pasta water. Add the piping hot pasta to the bowl with the pesto and toss it together well, making sure to melt the butter with the heat of the pasta. Continue to toss, adding a little pasta water at a time, until the sauce has thinned out a bit and is creamy.

Garnish the pasta with thin slivers of basil, a little sprinkling of grated Parmigiano-Reggiano, and/or a drizzle of extra-virgin olive oil, if you like.

ARCTIC CHAR WITH WHITE SOY VINAIGRETTE

WITH *potatoes, wax beans, radishes, and jalapeños*

SERVES 4 TO 6

I absolutely love this dish for its versatility: It's built around the white soy vinaigrette, which is full of great flavors. That's why you can substitute just about anything: the type of fish—though I love the flavor of Arctic char—another crunchy vegetable for the radishes, or asparagus instead of beans. I usually keep the potatoes, and try to use fingerlings, as they're creamier and sweeter than most others. White soy sauce is lesser known than regular soy sauce, but it's easily found at Asian markets, often labeled "light soy sauce." It has a different flavor, because it is usually brewed with more wheat or other grains, so you can't sub in dark soy sauce here.

TIP *Feel free to leave the seeds in the chile pepper if you want some extra heat.*

FOR THE VINAIGRETTE

1/3	cup (75 ml) rice wine vinegar
1/3	cup (75 ml) white soy sauce
1/4	cup (60 ml) fresh lime juice
2	tablespoons brown sugar
1	tablespoon finely chopped garlic
1	tablespoon finely chopped peeled fresh ginger
1	tablespoon finely chopped pickled jalapeño chile (or use 1 fresh Thai bird's eye chile)
1/2	cup (120 ml) grapeseed oil
1	tablespoon sesame oil
	Kosher salt and freshly ground black pepper

FOR THE FISH

4	Arctic char fillets (6 ounces/170 g each), patted dry
	Kosher salt and freshly ground black pepper
1	tablespoon grapeseed oil

FOR THE SALAD

1	pound (455 g) fingerling potatoes, cut into 1/2-inch (12-mm) rounds and roasted or blanched
1/2	pound (225 g) wax or green beans, cut in half and blanched
5	small radishes, thinly sliced
1	large jalapeño chile, seeded and thinly sliced
2	scallions, thinly sliced on the bias
1/2	cup (20 g) fresh cilantro leaves

Make the vinaigrette: In a blender or food processor, combine the vinegar, soy sauce, lime juice, brown sugar, garlic, ginger, and chile and pulse to combine. With the machine running, slowly add in both oils. Season with salt if necessary and plenty of black pepper. Set aside.

Make the fish: Season the fillets with salt and pepper. In a skillet large enough to hold the fillets without crowding them, heat the grapeseed oil over medium-high heat. When the oil shimmers, add the fillets to the pan skin side down.

Cook the fish until a nice crust forms on the skin, about 3 minutes, then flip them over; cook for 1 minute more and turn off the heat. Let the fillets sit in the hot pan while you make the salad. (This produces fillets that are just shy of fully cooked through, which I prefer. If you prefer them well done, cook the fish for a minute or two longer.)

Make the salad: In a large bowl, toss together the potatoes, beans, radishes, chile, scallions, and cilantro. Add enough vinaigrette to coat the vegetables liberally. (Don't be shy with the vinaigrette, as it will also serve as the sauce for the fish.)

Serve each fillet topped with an ample portion of salad and vinaigrette.

QUINOA-STUFFED SQUID

WITH *mango salsa* AND *inky butter sauce*

SERVES 4 TO 6

I love this dish, though it didn't do that well at The Good Fork as a special. Even though squid is sustainable, affordable, easily found fresh instead of chemically treated and frozen, and really tastes good, it's a hard sell. That's one of the reasons I stuffed it with two colors of quinoa. This was back when the quinoa craze was just beginning, and its simple, earthy flavor is just what I wanted for this dish. I added the squid ink to the sauce for its dramatic appearance—it's black!—and it really elevates the dish. With the yellow, green, and orange of the mango salsa, this is an impressive plate to put out on the table for a party.

> **TIP** *You can usually get squid ink from a good-quality fishmonger. Ask them to clean the squid, too, keeping the tubes intact so you can stuff them, and to be sure to save the tentacles, as you'll need them.*

FOR THE **MANGO SALSA**

- 2 plum tomatoes, finely diced
- 1 mango, finely diced
- 1 small red onion, finely minced
- 3 tablespoons fresh lime juice
- 1 serrano chile, minced
- 2 tablespoons chopped fresh cilantro
- 1 tablespoon fish sauce

FOR THE **STUFFED SQUID**

- 1 cup (170 g) red quinoa
- 1 cup (170 g) white quinoa
  Kosher salt
- 2 small shallots, minced
- 6 tablespoons (90 ml) extra-virgin olive oil
- 1/4 cup (60 ml) fresh lemon juice
- 2 tablespoons whole-grain Dijon mustard
- 2 tablespoons red wine vinegar
- 1 tablespoon maple syrup
- 3 tablespoons chopped fresh parsley
- 12 medium fresh squid, cleaned
- 12 toothpicks

FOR THE **INK SAUCE**

- 1 cup (240 ml) shrimp or seafood stock
- 3 tablespoons squid ink
- 2 tablespoons cold unsalted butter, cut into 2 pieces

RECIPE FOLLOWS

Make the mango salsa: In a medium bowl, combine the tomatoes, mango, onion, lime juice, chile, cilantro, and fish sauce. Adjust the seasoning with salt to taste, and refrigerate until ready to use.

Make the squid: Rinse and drain both colors of quinoa, then put them in a pot large enough to let the grains double in volume. Add 1 quart (960 ml) water and ½ teaspoon salt. Cover the pot, bring the quinoa to a boil, then turn the heat to low and let it simmer for 15 minutes. Turn off the heat but leave the pot covered for 5 more minutes, then uncover and fluff the quinoa with a fork.

In a large mixing bowl, combine the shallots, olive oil, lemon juice, mustard, vinegar, maple syrup, and 1½ teaspoons salt. Add the quinoa and toss to season it evenly. Mix in the parsley. Taste the quinoa salad for seasoning and add up to another ½ teaspoon salt—you want it to be well-seasoned since it will be stuffed inside the squid.

Fill each squid body with quinoa salad and pin it closed with a toothpick. Set aside.

Heat a gas or charcoal grill or a stovetop grill pan to very high heat—you want it very hot to quickly cook the squid—or preheat your broiler.

Meanwhile, make the base for the ink sauce: In a small saucepan over high heat, bring the stock and squid ink to a boil. Turn down the heat and simmer the sauce until it is reduced by half, about 12 minutes. Set aside.

When your grill is hot, brush it with oil, or grease the pan you will broil the squid on. Grill or broil the squid, turning once after 3 or 4 minutes, until it feels firm and bouncy.

Warm the ink sauce over low heat and whisk in the butter. Ladle a small amount onto a plate, then top it with 2 or 3 squid and some mango salsa, drizzling both with a little more ink sauce.

SALT-BROILED MACKEREL

WITH *daikon* AND *frisée salad*

SERVES 4

This is my all-time favorite simple and easy dinner. Mackerel is my ideal fish, because it has such a meaty, deep flavor. It's an oily fish, which means it is also high in omega-3 fatty acids. They make a version of this dish all over Japan and Korea; I ate many similar meals before I moved to the States—because there's so much of these cheaper fish that nobody wants to eat in the West. Over the past decade, though, I've noticed that many Americans have come around to my way of thinking, and sardines, mackerel, and bluefish are gaining notice.

TIP *The fish by itself is good on a nice bowl of steamed brown rice, too.*

FOR THE MACKEREL

Vegetable oil or cooking spray

2 skin-on mackerel fillets (6 to 8 ounces/ 170 to 225 g each)

Kosher salt

1 tablespoon gochujang (Korean red chile paste; see page 21)

1 clove garlic, minced

1 teaspoon grated peeled fresh ginger

1 tablespoon rice wine vinegar

1 teaspoon honey

1 teaspoon sesame oil

1 lemon, cut into wedges (optional)

FOR THE SALAD

1 tablespoon rice wine vinegar

1 teaspoon soy sauce

1 teaspoon fish sauce

1 teaspoon sesame oil

½ teaspoon gochujaru (Korean dried red pepper flakes; see page 21)

2 cups (95 grams) bite-size pieces frisée lettuce

1 cup (135 grams) thinly sliced daikon radish

⅓ cup (20 g) thinly sliced scallions, green parts only

Make the mackerel: Preheat the broiler.

With the oil or cooking spray, grease a baking sheet. Salt the flesh and skin of the mackerel fillets generously. Cut shallow 1-inch (2.5-cm) slits all along the skin about 2 inches (5 cm) apart and set the fish aside for 30 minutes.

In a small bowl, whisk together the gochujang, garlic, ginger, vinegar, honey, and sesame oil, and set aside.

Make the salad dressing: In a small bowl or jar, combine the vinegar, soy sauce, fish sauce, sesame oil, and gochujaru. Set aside.

Pat the salted fish fillets dry and broil them skin side up for 4 minutes, or until the skin begins to blister. Brush the gochujang sauce onto the skin, reserving some for garnishing the dish, and broil for 1 minute more, or until the skin is blistered, crisp, and slightly charred in spots. Set aside to rest while you make the salad.

In a large mixing bowl, toss the frisée, daikon, and scallions in the dressing until the leaves are coated. (Do not dress the salad until ready to serve, or it will become soggy.)

Serve each fillet on a pool of some additional sauce with a side of salad and a lemon wedge, if using.

TROUT

WITH *mushroom succotash* AND *lemon beurre blanc*

SERVES 4

I made this dish up for Ben. He told me that once, when he was small, he was traveling with his family in Europe and they ate at a tiny little French bistro where he had the most amazing piece of fish with beurre blanc. His parents are great cooks: When we were dating, we would go over to their house for crazy-tasty multicourse meals (still do), but he would always talk about how real chefs make all these traditional sauces. He is right—beurre blanc is a great classic French sauce, and it requires just a little finesse. Ben's French uncle, Pierre, complimented me on this dish, so you know it's good. It's all about the balance of fat and acid. I paired it with trout, which is one of my favorite fish because of its meaty texture. You can make it with any flaky white fish, though, as well as any fresh seasonal vegetables.

FOR THE SUCCOTASH

7	ounces (210 g) fresh maitake mushrooms, broken into large bite-size pieces
	Kosher salt
2	tablespoons canola oil
2	tablespoons unsalted butter
1	shallot, minced
3	ears fresh corn, kernels cut off the cob
1 1/2	cups (105 g) thinly sliced bias-cut baby bok choy or tatsoi
	Freshly ground black pepper
1	teaspoon chopped fresh tarragon
1	tablespoon thinly sliced scallion
	Fresh chervil or parsley leaves, for garnish (optional)

FOR THE LEMON BEURRE BLANC

1	cup (240 ml) white wine
1	shallot, diced
1	teaspoon black peppercorns
2	teaspoons fresh lemon juice
4	tablespoons (1/2 stick/55 g) cold unsalted butter, cut into small pieces
	Kosher salt and freshly ground black pepper

FOR THE FISH

2	tablespoons canola oil
4	trout pieces (6 ounces/170 g each)

RECIPE FOLLOWS

Make the succotash: Preheat the oven to 450°F (230°C) and grease a baking sheet.

In a bowl, toss the mushrooms with ¼ teaspoon salt, spread them out on the baking sheet, and roast them for 10 minutes. Set aside.

In a skillet, heat the oil and butter over medium-high heat, then cook the shallots until they barely begin to color, about 2 minutes. Add the corn kernels and sauté them until slightly browned, about 3 minutes. Add the bok choy and cook just until it is tender.

Transfer the vegetables to a bowl, fold in the roasted mushrooms, and season with salt and pepper. Mix in the tarragon and scallion, and set the bowl aside while you make the beurre blanc.

Make the beurre blanc: In a small pot or pan, combine the wine, shallot, and peppercorns and simmer over medium heat until the mixture reduces to a thick glaze; you want it to yield about 2 tablespoons.

Strain out the peppercorns and shallots and return the sauce to the pan. Stir in the lemon juice, and, working over very low heat, whisk in small pieces of cold butter until the sauce is thick and emulsified. Season with salt and pepper and keep warm while you cook the trout.

Make the trout: In a sauté pan, heat the canola oil over high heat. Cook the fish for 3 minutes on each side, or until slightly brown and crispy around the edges, then serve over the succotash with the beurre blanc on top. Garnish the dish with parsley or chervil, if using.

SAUTÉED SKATE

WITH *sauce amandine* AND *fennel-onion confit*

SERVES 4

In addition to a beurre blanc, I also like a classic French bistro *amandine* sauce, which is essentially a lot of butter, lemon, and almonds. It's old school, simple, and delicious. Sometimes all a really great fish needs is a simple sauce and some delicious vegetables, in this case fennel and onions. There's no twist on this recipe to make it particularly Good Fork in style, but I learned that it doesn't need it, as this was always a big hit at the restaurant. For home cooks, it's both a solid weeknight dinner and good enough for guests on the weekends. Just don't skimp on the butter or the lemon juice.

> **TIP** *Don't be intimidated by the word* confit. *Confit technically means any food that is slowly cooked in fat or sugar so that it is preserved—in this case, we're braising the vegetables in wine, too.*

FOR THE FENNEL-ONION CONFIT

2   tablespoons unsalted butter
1   large onion, sliced from root to stem ½ inch (12 mm) thick
8   cloves garlic, minced
3   large fennel bulbs, cored and sliced lengthwise into ½-inch (12-mm) sticks
2   tablespoons fennel seeds, toasted and ground
1   teaspoon crushed red pepper flakes
1   to 1 ½ cups (240 to 360 ml) white wine

FOR THE SAUCE AMANDINE

4   tablespoons (½ stick/55 g) unsalted butter
⅓   cup (30 g) sliced almonds, toasted
2   tablespoons chopped fresh parsley, plus extra for garnish
1   tablespoon fresh lemon juice
     Kosher salt and freshly ground black pepper

FOR THE FISH

2   tablespoons grapeseed or canola oil
4   skate fillets (6 to 7 ounces/170 to 200 g each), patted dry
     Kosher salt and freshly ground black pepper

Make the fennel-onion confit: In a large skillet, melt the butter over medium-low heat, then cook the onion, garlic, and fennel until they soften but do not brown, about 10 minutes.

Raise the heat to medium, add the ground fennel seeds and chile flakes, and cook, stirring, for a minute or two.

Add the wine, scraping up any bits at the bottom of the pan. Cook until the wine is a sauce-like consistency and the vegetables are just cooked through but not mushy, about 10 minutes. Keep warm.

Make the sauce: In a medium skillet, melt the butter over high heat until it begins to brown and foam. When the foam subsides and the butter is brown and nutty—this happens fast, in about a minute and a half—turn off the heat. Stir in the toasted almonds, parsley, and lemon juice and season with salt and pepper.

Make the fish: Heat a large skillet over medium-high heat until is very hot. Add the oil to the pan and swirl the pan so that the oil coats the bottom.

Season the fillets with salt and pepper, place them skin side down in the pan, and cook them until they begin to brown, 2 to 3 minutes. Flip the fillets over, turn off the heat, and let the fillets continue to cook in the pan for 2 minutes more, or until they are cooked through.

To serve the dish, top the fillets with a generous pool of sauce amandine, serve with a side of fennel-onion confit, and garnish with additional parsley.

MISO CARAMEL ICE CREAM

SERVES 4 TO 6

Before my ice cream maker crapped out at The Good Fork, we were coming up with ice cream flavors all the time. One day, when my line cook Yong—who is now my partner at Insa, our Korean barbecue restaurant—suggested we make miso butterscotch for a dessert, I realized it would make a great ice cream. (Though technically, we're making caramel rather than butterscotch because we're using white sugar rather than brown.) If you don't feel like making ice cream, you can of course use the miso caramel on anything you like.

FOR THE MISO CARAMEL

- ⅓ cup (65 g) sugar
- ¼ cup (60 ml) cream
- 1 tablespoon unsalted butter
- ⅓ cup (75 ml) shiro (white) miso

FOR THE ICE CREAM BASE

- ⅓ cup (65 g) sugar
- 5 egg yolks
- 2 cups (480 ml) whole milk
- 1 cup (240 ml) heavy cream
- 1 teaspoon vanilla extract

Make the miso caramel: In a small saucepan, combine the sugar with ¼ cup (60 ml) water and cook them over medium heat, watching the entire time. Do not stir, but swirl the pan occasionally. When the mixture froths up, then turns light golden brown, whisk in the cream and then the butter. Whisk in the miso, and set the miso caramel aside while you make the ice cream base.

Make the ice cream: In a medium bowl, whisk together the sugar and egg yolks until pale and frothy and set them aside.

In a medium pot over medium-high heat, gently warm the milk and cream until it just reaches a simmer, stirring with a rubber spatula to ensure the bottom doesn't scorch.

Whisk 1 cup (240 ml) of the warm cream mixture into the egg yolks, then add the tempered mixture back into the pot. Reduce the heat to medium-low and gently stir with a wooden spatula until it reaches a custard-like consistency, the mixture coats a spoon, and a finger swiped across the spoon will leave a clean trail.

Whisk in the miso caramel and the vanilla, then strain the custard into a bowl. Cover it with plastic wrap and refrigerate until completely cooled. Churn according to your ice cream maker's instructions.

DOUBLE-CHOCOLATE CUSTARD TART

SERVES 6 TO 8

A story that illustrates just how little Ben and I care about sweets is the one about when we saved up for a trip and ate at Taillevent, a three-Michelin-star restaurant in France where we spent $400 we couldn't afford on a multicourse lunch. I think we had fifteen, eighteen courses. Even so, when we got close to dessert, Ben asked if he could skip it and have foie gras instead, much to our waiter's horror. And we did! At our restaurant, well, I've already told you that I'm an uninspired pastry chef. I don't really have the patience to create much beyond the few basic recipes that I mastered early on. But I know what I like—something simple, with chocolate—and that's where our sous chef Rigo comes in. He has a real finesse with dessert, and he helped me nail this excellent tart with a bittersweet custard and a pleasingly crumbly crust that I continue to serve today, as well as many other desserts, like the Flan-Impossible Cake (page 140).

TIP *I serve this either sprinkled with Maldon sea salt or with whipped cream and fresh berries.*

FOR THE CHOCOLATE CRUST

1 1/4	cups (155 g) all-purpose flour
1/4	cup (25 g) unsweetened cocoa powder
2	tablespoons sugar
1/2	teaspoon kosher salt
10	tablespoons (1 1/4 sticks/140 g) cold unsalted butter, cut into small pieces and slightly softened

FOR THE CHOCOLATE CUSTARD

3/4	cup (180 ml) heavy cream
1/3	cup (75 ml) whole milk
2	tablespoons sugar
1/4	teaspoon kosher salt
4 1/2	ounces (130 g) 70% bittersweet chocolate, roughly chopped
1	large egg
1	teaspoon vanilla extract

Make the crust: In a large mixing bowl, combine the flour, cocoa powder, sugar, and salt. Using a fork, your fingers, or a food processor, blend in the butter until the dough comes together to form a ball. If the dough feels too sticky to work with, wrap it in plastic and refrigerate it for 20 to 30 minutes.

Grease a 9½-inch (24-cm) tart pan. Cover the top of the dough with a sheet of plastic wrap, and then use your fingers to press the dough—using the plastic wrap as a barrier—into the pan, spreading it out evenly on the bottom and sides. With a knife, scrape off any excess dough overhanging the sides. Refrigerate until firm, about 40 minutes.

Meanwhile, preheat the oven to 400°F (205°C). Bake the tart shell for 15 minutes, or until it darkens in color and looks dry, then let it cool completely on a wire rack. Adjust the oven temperature to 325°F (165°C).

Make the custard: In a heavy-bottomed saucepan, heat the cream, milk, sugar, and salt over medium-high heat until the mixture steams but does not boil. Turn off the heat, stirring to make sure the sugar is dissolved. Add the chocolate, stirring until it is melted and smooth, and set aside.

In a medium mixing bowl, beat the egg. Pour about ½ cup (120 ml) of the chocolate mixture into the egg and whisk it together. Gradually whisk in the rest of the chocolate mixture and then the vanilla. This is your custard.

Pour the custard into the cooled chocolate shell, place it on a baking sheet, and bake for 25 minutes, or until the filling is just barely set. Let it cool on a wire rack, then refrigerate until firm enough to slice and serve, at least 1 hour.

FLAN-IMPOSSIBLE CAKE

WITH *goat's milk cajeta*

SERVES 8 TO 10

This is another contribution from our old friend Rigo. This is a really cool one: You make it by layering *cajeta*—the Mexican version of dulce de leche, often made with goat's milk—then chocolate cake and flan. But in the end, you flip it out of the loaf pan, and it's flan, chocolate, and a sweet-tangy topping of cajeta. It's really gorgeous, and it's mainly chocolate cake, which you already know I love. You can double the cajeta recipe if you want to make extra: It keeps indefinitely in the refrigerator. Conversely, you could use 1 cup (240 ml) store-bought cajeta, dulce de leche, or caramel sauce. You'll also want to plan ahead to make this, as you need to refrigerate the cake after it has cooled for at least four hours.

> **TIP** *Save the pods from your vanilla beans to make vanilla sugar. Tuck them into a sugar bowl and let it sit until the sugar takes on the scent and flavor of the pods.*

FOR THE CAJETA

2	cups (480 ml) goat's milk or whole cow's milk
1/2	cup (100 g) sugar
	Kosher salt
1/8	teaspoon baking soda

FOR THE CHOCOLATE CAKE

	Canola oil or cooking spray
3/4	cup (95 g) all-purpose flour
1/3	cup (30 g) unsweetened cocoa powder
1/2	cup (100 g) sugar
1	teaspoon kosher salt
1/2	teaspoon baking soda
1/4	teaspoon baking powder
1/2	cup (120 ml) buttermilk
1	large egg
3	tablespoons canola oil
1	teaspoon vanilla extract

FOR THE FLAN

4	large eggs
1	can evaporated milk (14 ounces/400 g)
1	can sweetened condensed milk (14 ounces/400 g)
1/2	teaspoon ground cinnamon
1	vanilla bean
	Hot water

RECIPE FOLLOWS

Make the cajeta: In a small, heavy-bottomed pan or double boiler, combine the milk, sugar, and salt. Bring the milk to a simmer, then whisk in the baking soda. Simmer very gently, stirring occasionally, for about 45 minutes. As the mixture becomes thick and golden, stir more frequently, then constantly, until it is the color and texture of a caramel sauce. If it's too thick, add a little water; if it's too thin, keep cooking. (Don't worry about lumps; most will dissolve, and you can always push the finished mixture through a sieve if it is very lumpy.) Remove from the heat and set aside.

Make the cake: Preheat the oven to 375°F (190°C) and grease a large loaf pan with the oil or cooking spray. Spread 1 cup (240 ml) of the cajeta on the bottom of the pan and set it aside.

In a large mixing bowl, whisk together the flour, cocoa powder, sugar, salt, baking soda, and baking powder. In a small mixing bowl, whisk together the buttermilk, egg, canola oil, and vanilla. Add them to the dry ingredients, mixing until just combined. Pour the batter into the cake pan over the cajeta and set it aside while you make the flan.

Make the flan: In another large mixing bowl or the jar of a blender, beat the eggs. Add the evaporated milk, condensed milk, and cinnamon. Scrape the vanilla bean seeds into the bowl, then whisk or blend to combine everything thoroughly. Gently pour the flan over the cake batter.

Place the cake pan inside a roasting pan and fill the roasting pan with a few inches of hot water, or as high as you can without it sloshing over the sides of the roasting pan. Cover the cake loosely with foil and bake it for 50 minutes, or until the flan is set (it will still be a little wobbly, but because you chill it, it will be fine).

Cool the cake completely, then refrigerate it for at least 4 hours or overnight. Run a knife around the edges of the cake, then turn it out of the pan. Slice and serve.

ESSAY

PATTY GENTRY, EARLY GIRL FARM

I have known Patty Gentry since long before she was our farmer. In fact, she cooked at The Good Fork for three months. It was right after we got reviewed in the *New York Times*, and I went from thirty or forty dinners a night to sixty, seventy, then eighty. I needed another line cook, and Patty answered my online ad.

I was floored: She had way more experience than I did. She had been a head chef at incredible Manhattan restaurants, had launched her own business—the Hampton Chutney Co.—then sold it and worked as a consultant. "Why on earth would you want to come here?" I asked her. She replied, "I read your post and it really moved me. I felt your heart, I felt your soul." That's Patty.

As it turns out, Patty was looking for her next step; she told me she was tired of being a chef and was ready to go further, to be a part of where it all comes from. "I don't want to use the best ingredients," she told me, "I want to grow them." She needed a placeholder while she figured out what to do next. I was like, "Okay, it's yours!"

For me, it felt like Patty was—pardon the cheesiness—an angel sent from heaven at just the right time. It was like Yoda was working for me, and I was Luke Skywalker: "No! Try not! Do or do not. There is no try."

She just had this way of guiding me to be better, which is what I really needed right at that point. "This is a great dish," she would tell me, "but we have to get it out faster," and then she'd show me how. I thought I knew what I was doing, but I had only worked as a cook for six years at that point, and there was a lot left to learn about running a kitchen—about running a restaurant.

Patty also verbalized what I already felt—she told me that The Good Fork felt like a family, and that we needed to strengthen that feeling, which helped crystallize what type of place we were going to be for those who worked and cooked there.

The shocking thing was that when I look back, Patty made such an impact, but she only worked with us for a few months before she went home to Long Island to learn to farm from some of the best: "I'm going to have my own stuff," she said, "and I'm going to give it to you." She learned how to grow some of the most incredible vegetables and curate some of the most viable, rich soil in a part of the state already known for great farmland.

Her farm—which is called Early Girl Farm—is currently on a one-acre parcel of land owned by the one and only Isabella Rossellini. What makes her an especially great farmer—one whose fiery, gnarled *cigaretto de bergamo* chiles, deep purple Mitoyo eggplants, or skinny, snakelike Armenian cucumbers are coveted by some of the city's best chefs, whom she hand-picks to sell to—is her approach to tending to the soil. Her stuff is scattered all over our menu. I take pictures of all of the produce she sends west to me, often bringing it by herself. Do we have it all year long? No, but from May to November, it's just bliss.

FARM SALAD VINAIGRETTE
chez schneider

1 CUP (240 ML)

This is the simple, easy vinaigrette my amazing parents-in-law taught me a decade and a half ago, which I now serve with my farm salad—made of whichever greens and crunchy vegetables I am lucky enough to get from Patty Gentry that week. Anyone who's been lucky enough to have Peter and Jane cook for them at Chez Schneider has tasted this already. They always serve an amazing salad at the end of the meal to cut the fat and to cleanse the palate. The peanut oil is key!

$\frac{1}{3}$ cup (75 ml) white balsamic vinegar
$\frac{1}{3}$ cup (75 ml) peanut oil
$\frac{1}{4}$ cup (60 ml) extra-virgin olive oil
2   cloves garlic, minced
1   teaspoon Dijon mustard
$\frac{1}{4}$ teaspoon kosher salt
3   or 4 grinds freshly ground black pepper

In a jar with a lid, combine the vinegar, oils, garlic, mustard, salt, and pepper and shake until the dressing is thick and emulsified. This lasts in the fridge for at least a week.

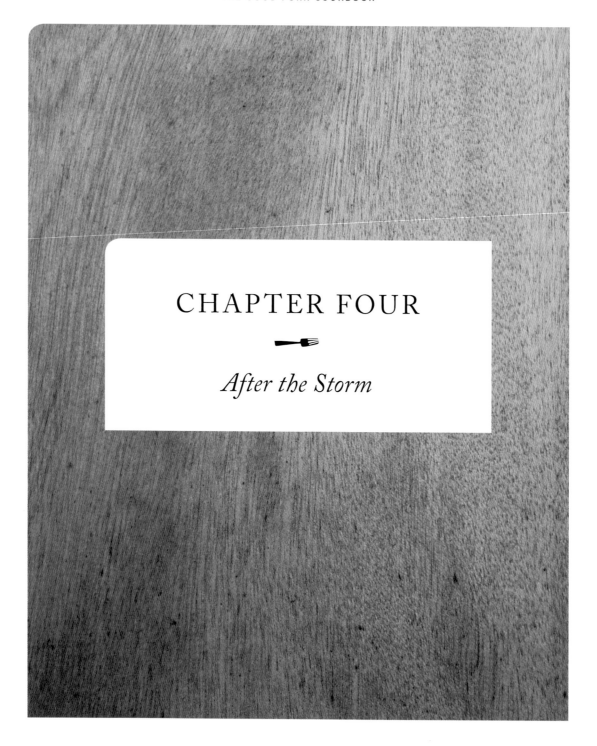

CHAPTER FOUR

After the Storm

HURRICANE SANDY NEARLY WIPED OUT our neighborhood on October 29, 2012, and The Good Fork was no exception. There were several feet of water in our dining room, our basement was submerged, and between cleanup and loss of revenue, the cold winter months after the storm were even harder than the initial opening. In typical Red Hook fashion, the neighborhood bonded together to help one another rebuild and stay sane through the whole ordeal. Our family, customers, neighbors, and staff showed an immense outpouring of love and support until we were able to open the doors again on New Year's Eve.

I decided that our reopening was a going to be a reboot, a do-over. My kids were a little older, and I was back at work full-time with a resurgence of ideas and creativity. Honestly, I wanted to scrap our whole menu and start from scratch. But Ben brought me back to earth. So I kept our signatures but reworked the rest. For starters, we added a serious brunch—I loved working with our new brunch crew to think up recipes like biscuits with gochujang-honey butter and my own yogurt with black sesame granola. We also added ramen nights and summer specials, like the ribs I'd been making at home forever now paired with a savory bread pudding.

Shortly after our reopening, one of my former cooks—Sam Filloramo— came back to our kitchen. When Sam first came to work with us, not long after we opened in 2006, he didn't have much professional experience. But something about him made me think that he could learn. Ben really liked him, too. "Save your money on cooking school," I told Sam, "I will teach you what I know, but you have to promise to stay for at least a year."

He did. And when Sam asked if he could "come home," he had been working at other really good restaurants, many with lots of acclaim. Plus, Sam met his wife, Meg Bouchard, here—she's worked alongside us since the beginning. Their son, Rocco, is one bona fide Buona Forchetta baby! (You can see Sam and Meg on page 13.)

Ben and I were already thinking about doing another project, which would later become Insa. So we knew we'd eventually need a new head chef for The Good Fork. It felt right that it would be Sam—an extended family member.

SHRIMP AND GRITS

WITH *chimichurri*

SERVES 4

When I think of brunch, I think hangover food—cravings for things that are fried or smothered. So I wanted something that was globe-trotting in the spirit of The Good Fork, but still gave people what they wanted on a weekend morning. This dish is obviously inspired by the South Carolina classic, but our chimichurri, a Latin American salsa made with herbs and chiles, was created by my longstanding sous chef Rigo, who drew on his knowledge of Mexican sauce- and salsa-making. We also went with a lemony marinade for the shrimp, instead of cooking them in the sauce, so the dish has a little more brightness than you see in the original. It's key to use good-quality, fresh shrimp if you can get it—it's worth it in terms of flavor. Nothing is worse than rubbery, mushy shrimp when they're the main element of a dish.

> **TIP** *Note that when we make grits—we also use them with a braised pork shoulder instead of polenta—we always use good-quality stone-ground grits. Like dried beans, I soak them for 5 hours or overnight if they're very coarse, to shorten the cooking time from 50 minutes to 15. But Koreans soak everything, so I'm used to it. I remember in my mom's kitchen everything soaking—mung beans, dehydrated mushrooms, the cabbage for the kimchee. The easiest way to execute this dish is to soak the grits and marinate the shrimp the night before.*

FOR THE GRITS

1	cup (120 g) stone-ground coarse grits
1/4	cup (120 ml) milk
3	tablespoons unsalted butter
1	teaspoon salt

FOR THE SHRIMP

1	pound (455 g) large shrimp, peeled and deveined
1	lemon, zested (about 1 tablespoon zest)
2	cloves garlic, minced
2	sprigs fresh thyme, stems and leaves separated
	Freshly ground black pepper
2	tablespoons extra-virgin olive oil

FOR THE CHIMICHURRI

1/2	cup (25 g) minced chives
1/3	cup (17 g) minced fresh parsley
1/3	cup (45 g) minced shallots
4	canned pickled jalapeños, minced
2	tablespoons minced fresh mint
2	tablespoons fresh lime juice
2	tablespoons pickle juice
2	tablespoons minced scallion
1	tablespoon honey
1	large clove garlic, minced
1	teaspoon paprika

FOR THE PAN SAUCE

1/4	cup (60 ml) shrimp or chicken stock
2	tablespoons cold unsalted butter
	Chopped chives, parsley, or other fresh herbs for garnish

RECIPE FOLLOWS

Prep the grits: In a heavy-bottomed pot, soak the grits in 1 quart (960 ml) water for a few hours or overnight.

Marinate the shrimp: In a large bowl, combine the shrimp, lemon zest, garlic, thyme, pepper, and olive oil. Marinate, covered in the refrigerator, for at least 1 hour or overnight.

Make the chimichurri: In a medium bowl, combine the chives, parsley, shallots, jalapeños, mint, lime juice, pickle juice, scallion, honey, garlic, and paprika and mix well. Set aside.

Make the grits: In the soaking pot, bring the grits to a simmer in their soaking water and cook, stirring constantly, until they are tender, usually no more than 15 minutes. Stir in the milk and butter and season with the salt. Keep them warm while you make the shrimp.

Make the shrimp and sauce: In a medium saucepan, cook the shrimp over medium-high heat until just cooked through, 2 to 2½ minutes per side. Remove them from the pan and set them aside in a bowl, then add the stock to the pan. Bring the stock to a simmer and cook until it is reduced by half. Turn the heat to low, add the cold butter, and slowly blend it into the reduced stock.

To serve the dish, place a big spoonful of grits in a deep bowl, top with chimichurri, some shrimp, and then the sauce; garnish with fresh herbs. Serve immediately.

BUTTERMILK FRIED CHICKEN

AND *waffles*

SERVES 8

This was the second dish I knew I wanted for our brunch menu. We also do a Korean-style fried chicken that's dusted in cornstarch, but this is a classic, straight-up Southern approach—and who can resist perfectly fried chicken, especially with a waffle, at breakfast? A really good buttermilk fried chicken takes time: My friend, former cook and now farmer Patty Gentry, told me years ago that a proper fried chicken takes three days: one to salt it, one to soak it in seasoned buttermilk to really infuse the flavors, and one to fry it. We condense it to two steps at The Good Fork. It takes less time, but I think the three-day method can give you rubbery meat if you oversalt the bird. I serve this with some freshly macerated berries and dust the plate with a little bit of powdered sugar. Even on the fried chicken it's good; trust me!

FOR THE **CHICKEN**

8	chicken thighs, trimmed of extra fat
8	chicken drumsticks
1	to 2 cups (240 to 480 ml) buttermilk
2	tablespoons kosher salt
1	tablespoon Tabasco sauce
2	quarts (2 L) vegetable oil
1	cup (125 g) all-purpose flour
1	teaspoon freshly ground black pepper
	Generous pinch cayenne
½	teaspoon paprika

FOR THE **WAFFLES**

1	tablespoon active dry yeast
½	cup (120 ml) lukewarm water
½	cup (1 stick/115 g) unsalted butter
2	cups (480 ml) milk
2	cups (250 g) all-purpose flour
2	tablespoons sugar
2	teaspoons salt
2	large eggs, beaten
1 ½	teaspoons baking powder
	Maple syrup, fresh berries, and powdered sugar for garnish

RECIPE FOLLOWS

The night before you plan to fry the chicken, mix the buttermilk, salt, and Tabasco in a large nonreactive bowl or container, then add the chicken. It should be nearly submerged. Cover and refrigerate overnight.

Make the waffles: In a large bowl, mix the yeast with the water and let it stand while you prepare the rest of the ingredients. In a small saucepan, melt the butter over medium-low heat. Turn off the heat and add the milk. In a medium mixing bowl, whisk together the flour, sugar, and salt.

By now, the yeast should have produced a few bubbles. (If not, the water might have been too hot or the yeast was not active, and you'll need to start with fresh yeast.) Add the milk mixture and flour mixture to the bowl with the yeast, and whisk just to combine—you want a few lumps. Cover the bowl with plastic wrap and let it stand at room temperature for 2 hours, or until it has grown in size and is very bubbly. (You can refrigerate the batter overnight before continuing on to the next step, just let it come to room temperature before using.)

Make the chicken: In a heavy-bottomed pot or Dutch oven, heat the vegetable oil over medium heat until the temperature reaches 350°F (175°C) to 370°F (190°C) degrees—you will want to keep within that range as you fry the chicken. Set a wire rack in a baking sheet or line it with paper towels.

Meanwhile, in a colander over the sink, drain the chicken. In a mixing bowl, whisk together the flour, pepper, cayenne, and paprika. Toss each piece of chicken in the seasoned flour and let it dry on a wire rack or a plate for 10 minutes. Keep the extra flour mixture.

When the oil is hot enough and the chicken has rested, dredge the chicken pieces again in the remaining flour mixture and tap gently to shake off any excess flour.

Cook the thighs in batches so they do not crowd the pan, until they are dark golden brown, about 10 minutes. Then cook the drumsticks in batches until they are dark golden brown, about 9 minutes. Remove the chicken with tongs or a slotted spoon and drain it on the wire rack. Let the chicken rest for at least 5 minutes before serving, or keep it in the oven on warm while you make the waffles.

Once the waffle batter has risen, whisk in the eggs and baking powder. Cook the batter in a waffle iron according to the maker's instructions.

Serve the chicken on top of the waffles, garnished with maple syrup and fresh berries and a generous dusting of powdered sugar.

HOUSEMADE YOGURT

WITH *black sesame granola*

MAKES 2½ QUARTS (2.5 L) YOGURT; SERVES 10 TO 12

There's lots of great granola being made in our part of the world, but for our brunch I wanted to make it in-house—it's a lot cheaper and most people don't realize how easy it is to make. Our twist is the black sesame seeds, which add a cool color contrast. I started making yogurt for a similar reason: I didn't want to pay for the good stuff, so I got a really good culture—meaning a few tablespoons of really good yogurt—and made my own. I like to think of culturing yogurt at home as a matter of economics. Why not turn a little bit of yogurt into a lot overnight? Technically the Department of Health frowns on yogurt-making in a restaurant because you leave the warmed milk unrefrigerated in the danger zone for too long for their liking, but home cooks don't have to worry about them. Don't get freaked out about leaving dairy out: It's just good bacteria at work, which is good tasting and good for you, too!

FOR THE YOGURT

2	quarts (2 L) whole milk
½	cup (125 g) plain whole-milk yogurt

FOR THE GRANOLA

1	tablespoon canola oil or another neutral oil
4	cups (360 g) old-fashioned rolled oats
1	cup (130 g) hulled unsalted pumpkin seeds or pepitas
1	cup (140 g) unsalted sunflower seeds
1	cup blanched sliced (95 g) or slivered (110 g) almonds
3	tablespoons black sesame seeds
¾	cup (180 ml) maple syrup
½	cup (110 g) packed brown sugar
4	tablespoons (½ stick/55 g) unsalted butter
¼	cup (60 ml) sesame oil
2	teaspoons kosher salt

RECIPE FOLLOWS

Start the yogurt at least one day before you intend to serve it. First, clean your cooking vessel: Fill a very clean large pot halfway full with cold water, then swirl the water in the pot and drain it out. Do not dry the pot—there should be traces of water. (I have found that this helps keep the yogurt from sticking to the bottom of the pot.)

Add the milk and heat it over steady, medium-low heat to just below a full boil or when an instant-read thermometer reads 200 to 210°F (90 to 100°C), about 45 minutes.

Remove the pot from the heat and let it cool until the milk is 115°F (46°C), about 30 minutes, or until the milk is cool enough that you can hold your finger in it for 5 seconds.

Whisk in the yogurt. Cover the pot and place it in a warm part of the kitchen, such as in an oven with a pilot light or even better, on top of the refrigerator. Let the pot sit overnight.

The next morning, you should have 2 quarts (2 L) of yogurt. You can either strain out the whey that collects on top to make a thick

labne or Greek-style yogurt, or just whisk it back in. Refrigerate the yogurt in smaller containers for up to 2 weeks.

Make the granola: Preheat the oven to 325°F (165°C).

Grease a large mixing bowl and two rimmed baking sheets with the canola oil. In the bowl, combine the oats, pumpkin seeds, sunflower seeds, almonds, and sesame seeds.

In a small saucepan, combine the maple syrup, brown sugar, butter, sesame oil, and salt. Warm the mixture over medium-low heat, stirring occasionally, just until the butter melts. Pour the liquids over the oat mixture in the bowl, and stir to thoroughly coat the oats and seeds.

Spread the mixture out on the greased baking sheets in an even layer and bake until evenly browned—don't stir it—for 30 to 35 minutes. Let it cool completely, then break the granola chunks into pieces or loosely crumble it and serve. This will last for weeks in a tightly sealed container in a cool place.

CRÈME FRAÎCHE BISCUITS

WITH *gochujang-honey butter*

MAKES ABOUT 12 BISCUITS

I am proud of my biscuit recipe—they make great breakfast sandwiches, too—but what really makes this dish is the gochujang-honey butter. We started out blending it up for staff meals. We called it "crack sauce." This was actually long before hot honey was a mainstream thing, and before calling something "crack" was a thing. In fact, our original crack sauce was actually the Sriracha Aioli (page 38), but nowadays you can find that anywhere.

FOR THE GOCHUJANG-HONEY BUTTER

½   cup (1 stick/115 g) unsalted butter, softened

2   tablespoons gochujang (Korean red chile paste; see page 21)

2   tablespoons honey

FOR THE BISCUITS

5   cups (625 g) all-purpose flour, plus more for dusting

2   tablespoons baking powder

2   tablespoons sugar

1   tablespoon kosher salt

1   cup (2 sticks/225 g) unsalted butter, cut into ½-inch (12-mm) cubes, frozen

1   cup (240 ml) heavy cream

5   ounces (140 g) crème fraîche

3   large eggs

Make the honey butter: In a small bowl, mix together the butter, gochujang, and honey until smooth. Set aside.

Make the biscuits: Preheat the oven to 350°F (175°C) and line a large baking sheet with parchment paper.

In the bowl of a large food processor, combine the flour, baking powder, sugar, and salt. Add the frozen butter and pulse until the butter is the size of small peas and well covered with the flour mixture. Remove the flour-butter mixture to a large bowl, make a well in the center, and add the heavy cream, crème fraîche, and 2 beaten eggs. Stir it just until it comes together.

Remove the flour-butter-cream mixture to a floured surface and knead it together for about 1 minute. Roll it out into a 2-inch (5-cm)-thick slab, then flip the dough over and roll it out until it is about 1½ inches (4 cm) thick. Cut it with a clean glass or 2- to 3-inch (5- to 7.5-cm) biscuit ring and place the biscuits on the parchment-lined baking sheet, keeping about 2 to 3 inches (5 to 7.5 cm) between the biscuits.

Brush the tops of biscuits with the remaining egg, beaten, and bake until golden brown and cooked through, about 20 minutes. Serve the biscuits warm with the gochujang-honey butter.

CHILAQUILES

with *fried eggs* and *avocado*

SERVES 6

This extraordinary brunch dish, one of my favorites from our first breakfast menu, was brought to The Good Fork by our sous chef, Rigo, who grew up eating it in Mexico. *Chilaquiles* is a very traditional Mexican comfort food served for breakfast or lunch, found in many variations. Traditionally, it is topped with eggs, usually fried ones, and you can also add refried beans, as we did in the beginning, or simply serve it with some avocado slices and lots of Mexican *queso fresco*, a crumbly, salty fresh cheese with a nice acidity. If you can't find it, a crumbly feta or ricotta salata also works. At the restaurant, we deep-fry the tortillas—which tastes amazing—and I encourage you to try it, but I made this recipe a little easier for home cooks by letting you toast them in the oven. For the eggs, just fry them to your liking—or you could even scramble them, if you prefer.

FOR THE SAUCE

1	large onion, cut into eighths
5	cloves garlic, peeled
1	can (28 ounces/785 g) peeled whole tomatoes, drained but juice reserved
1	or 2 jalapeños
2	tablespoons olive oil
1	bunch fresh cilantro, well washed, a few stems reserved for garnish
	Kosher Salt

FOR THE TORTILLAS

30	(6-inch/15-cm) corn tortillas, cut into wedges
½	cup (120 ml) canola oil
2	teaspoons kosher salt

FOR THE FINISHED DISH

6	large eggs, fried
2	ripe avocados, thinly sliced
5	red radishes, thinly sliced
5	ounces (115 g) queso fresco, crumbled

Make the sauce: Preheat the oven to 450°F (230°C).

On a rimmed baking sheet, toss the onion, garlic, drained tomatoes, and whole chile(s) with the olive oil. Bake for 30 minutes, or until soft and slightly browned, and let cool.

Turn the oven down to 400°F (205°C).

Remove the stems from the chiles, then put all the roasted vegetables into a blender with the reserved tomato juice and the cilantro minus a few stems, for garnish. Puree until smooth, adding up to ½ cup (120 ml) water if the sauce is too thick. Taste for salt and set aside.

Make the tortillas: In a large mixing bowl, toss the tortilla wedges with the canola oil, making sure they are evenly coated. Sprinkle the wedges with the salt, tossing to coat, and bake them on a baking sheet in a single layer until they are beginning to brown on the bottom, 10 to 12 minutes. Flip them over, rotate the pan in the oven, and continue to cook for another 10 minutes or so, or until they are crisp and brown all over.

In your largest skillet, heat the sauce over medium-high heat. Toss the toasted tortillas with the sauce to coat. Transfer them to a serving dish or individual plates and top with the fried eggs, avocado, radish, queso fresco, and reserved cilantro.

LAMB OSSO BUCO

WITH *split peas* AND *pea shoots*

SERVES 4

This was a very popular dish created by our chef de cuisine, Sam, in the spring following what I like to call The Storm (Hurricane Sandy). He was inspired by spring lamb and spring peas. Osso buco is an Italian slow braise traditionally made with veal shanks balanced with a *gremolata*, a mix of chopped lemon zest, garlic, and parsley. So instead of veal shanks, he uses lamb, and the accompaniments to this version include a riff on the mean split pea soup Sam already makes—thickened and spiked with fresh spring peas—and a brightly flavored and colored pea shoot salad. It's one of many home runs for The Good Fork from Sam. Note: You should have your butcher cut and tie the shanks for you.

FOR THE LAMB SHANKS

4   pieces lamb shank, cut crosswise as for osso buco 11/2 inches (4 cm) thick and tied with twine
1   tablespoon kosher salt
2   tablespoons olive oil
1   large onion, diced
1   medium carrot, diced
1   medium parsnip, diced
1   head garlic, peeled and minced
2   anchovy fillets, rinsed and patted dry
1   cup (240 ml) red wine
1   cup (240 ml) white wine
1/2   cup red wine vinegar
1   can (14.5 ounces/111 g) whole tomatoes
2   tablespoons capers
2   to 3 cups (480 to 720 ml) chicken stock
1   sprig fresh rosemary
5   sprigs fresh thyme

FOR THE SPLIT PEA PUREE

3   tablespoons extra-virgin olive oil
1   large onion, finely diced
2   small carrots, finely diced
2   stalks celery, finely diced
3   cloves garlic, minced
    Kosher salt and freshly ground black pepper
2   cups (190 g) dried split peas
1   cup fresh (145 g) or frozen (135 g) sweet peas

FOR THE PEA SHOOT SALAD

2   cups (70 g) pea shoots
    Juice from 1/2 lemon (about 1 1/2 tablespoons)
    Kosher salt and freshly ground black pepper

Make the lamb: Preheat the oven to 275°F (135°C).

Liberally sprinkle the lamb with the salt. Lightly cover the bottom of a large Dutch oven with the olive oil and heat it over medium-high heat. Brown the shanks, working in batches if necessary, so as not to crowd the meat. As the lamb pieces brown, remove them from the pot and set them aside, keeping the fat in the pan.

In the same pan, sauté the onion, carrot, parsnip, garlic, and anchovies until they are fragrant, 5 to 7 minutes. Add both wines and the vinegar and cook until they have reduced by half.

Blend the tomatoes in their liquid in a blender or roughly chop them, then add both the tomatoes and their liquid to the pan along with the capers and chicken stock.

Return the lamb shanks to the pan, along with the rosemary and thyme. Bring the pot to a boil and then transfer it to the oven. Braise for about 2 hours, or until the meat is very tender but not yet falling off the bone. (Check them at 1½ hours, as they may finish early, or they may take as long as 2½ hours.)

Remove the shanks from the braising liquid. Strain out the solids and skim the fat from the braising liquid. Discard the fat and solids. Return the liquid and shanks to the pot.

Meanwhile, make the split pea puree: In a medium stockpot, heat the olive oil over medium-high heat and then sauté the onion, carrots, celery, and garlic with a pinch of salt until they are translucent, 7 to 10 minutes.

Add the split peas with 1 quart (960 ml) water. Bring the pot to a boil, reduce the heat to a simmer, and cook until the peas are falling apart, about 35 minutes. Add pepper to your liking at this point. Salt liberally to bring out the sweetness of the peas.

Just before serving, add the fresh peas, cooking them for a minute or two, until they are soft and cooked through, then turn off the heat and mash them lightly into the puree. Season with salt and pepper.

Make the salad: When you are ready to serve the dish, put the pea shoots in a small mixing bowl and dress them with the lemon juice and season with salt and pepper.

Serve the lamb shanks in a bowl over a pile of the warm split pea puree, garnished with the dressed pea shoots.

PAN-SEARED COD AND SQUID

WITH *romesco sauce, roasted Japanese eggplants,* AND *sautéed Swiss chard*

SERVES 4 TO 6

Patty Gentry, our former cook and now a farmer, put the seed for this dish in my head. She mentioned in passing one day after a delivery of vegetables that something would be good with a Spanish *romesco* sauce. I'd never made one before, but it is delicious—a rough blend of bread and nuts and amazing Spanish fire-roasted, pickled piquillo peppers. They're some of my favorite things. I knew I wanted to make it to serve with fish, and at the time I had this guy from Massachusetts bringing me line-caught cod his family fished. He'd shown up out of the blue, and his prices were good and his fish was great. I added squid and some Mediterranean-style vegetables, and it went on our second-round opening menu after Hurricane Sandy. It turned out to be a perfect combination and is one of those rare meals that works throughout every single season.

TIP *If you want to simplify this dish, feel free to omit the squid or skip the eggplant or Swiss chard. You'll be really happy with just the sauce and fish. You can also make them several hours in advance and simply warm them up once the fish is done.*

FOR THE ROMESCO SAUCE

⅓	cup (45 g) whole hazelnuts
½	cup (55 g) slivered almonds
	Extra-virgin olive oil
3	thick slices (90 g) ciabatta bread
5	cloves garlic, crushed
6	canned peeled tomatoes, drained (about 6 oz./180 g)
8	jarred or canned pickled piquillo peppers (about 7 oz/200 g)
1	teaspoon paprika
¼	teaspoon cayenne pepper
2	tablespoons sherry wine vinegar
½	teaspoon kosher salt
	Roasted Japanese Eggplants (recipe follows)
	Sautéed Swiss Chard (recipe follows)

FOR THE FISH AND SQUID

8	ounces (225 g) medium squid, cleaned
4	cod fillets (6 ounces/170 g each)
	Kosher salt
2	tablespoons extra-virgin olive oil
1	lemon, halved
	Chopped fresh parsley leaves, for garnish

Make the romesco: Preheat the oven to 350°F (175°C).

Spread the hazelnuts out on one rimmed baking sheet and the almonds on another, and roast them for 10 minutes, or until they begin to brown and smell toasted. Set the almonds aside to cool and cover the hazelnuts with a dish towel until they are cool enough to touch. Roll them in the towel or your hands to remove the skins—they should come off easily. Discard the skins and set the nuts aside.

In a large skillet, heat about ¼ inch (6 mm) olive oil over medium-high heat and toast the ciabatta slices on both sides until they are dark golden brown, about 3 minutes. Remove the bread from the pan and set it aside, then turn the heat down to medium and add the garlic, cooking it until it begins to brown. Add the tomatoes, cook for 10 minutes more, then remove the pan from the heat.

In a food processor, roughly chop the nuts. Add the toasted bread, tomatoes, piquillo peppers, paprika, cayenne, sherry vinegar, and salt. With the motor running, pour in ¼ cup (60 ml) olive oil and process until it is fairly smooth, like a loose pesto. Add up to ¼ cup (60 ml) water to loosen the sauce so it will spread easily.

Spread the romesco on a large serving platter. Arrange the roasted eggplants and sautéed Swiss chard in small groupings on the platter, leaving room for the fish, before you make the fish and squid.

To make the fish and squid: Cut the squid bodies into rings. Season the rings, tentacles, and cod well with salt and set aside.

In a large skillet over high heat, warm the olive oil. When the oil shimmers, add the fish fillets and cook until the fish flakes easily with a fork, 2 to 3 minutes on each side. Transfer the fish to the serving platter with the sauce and vegetables.

Working in the same pan, cook the squid over high heat until just opaque and firm, about 1 minute. Turn off the heat and transfer the squid to the platter with the fish.

Squeeze the juice from the lemon over the platter—start with half a lemon and add more to taste—and sprinkle with parsley. Serve immediately.

SAUTÉED SWISS CHARD

SERVES 4 TO 6

Swiss chard is really best treated as two vegetables: The stems, which require longer cooking, and the leaves, which need only a minute or two. Most people throw away the stems, but they're worth the extra effort. Just listen to Ben's French uncle, Pierre, who always says, "You Americans are so crazy; you throw away the best part."

1	bunch Swiss chard
1	tablespoon olive oil
3	cloves garlic, roughly chopped
½	cup (120 ml) chicken stock
	Kosher salt

Separate the stems and leaves of the chard and roughly chop the stems. In a skillet, heat the oil over medium-high heat; add the garlic and chopped chard stems. Add the stock and ½ teaspoon salt, and simmer until the mixture reduces, about 5 minutes. Add the chard greens and cook for 2 minutes more. Season with salt to taste.

ROASTED JAPANESE EGGPLANTS

SERVES 4 TO 6

2	Japanese eggplants, cut into ½-inch (12-mm)-thick sticks
3	tablespoons extra-virgin olive oil
½	teaspoon kosher salt

Preheat the oven to 450°F (230°C).

On a baking sheet, toss the eggplant with the oil and salt. Roast until soft and nicely browned, 15 to 20 minutes. Keep warm until ready to serve.

WILD STRIPED BASS

IN *sweet onion curry sauce* WITH *black rice*

SERVES 4 TO 6

Good curry is a very satisfying dish to make. I love the Indian method of "blooming" spices, or toasting them to bring out the aromatics and levels of flavor before you make a dish. But I wanted this recipe to be a little simpler, to prove that good curry doesn't have to be totally complicated.

TIP *Garam masala is an Indian spice mix. The better quality and fresher the blend you buy, the better your results will be.*

FOR THE CURRY

4	tablespoons (½ stick/55 g) unsalted butter
2	large sweet onions, diced
2	tablespoons minced garlic
1	tablespoon minced peeled fresh ginger
½	teaspoon fennel seeds
3	cardamom pods
1	teaspoon coriander seeds
1	teaspoon cumin seeds
1	tablespoon tomato paste
⅓	cup (75 ml) white wine
⅓	cup (75 ml) heavy cream
⅓	cup (75 ml) chicken stock
1	tablespoon good-quality garam masala
1	teaspoon Madras curry powder
⅛	teaspoon cayenne pepper
1	teaspoon kosher salt
1	teaspoon fresh lime juice

FOR THE FISH

1 ½	cups black rice
4	wild striped bass fillets (6 ounces/170 g each), patted dry
	Kosher salt and freshly ground black pepper
	Grapeseed oil
2	tablespoons unsalted butter
	Cilantro leaves, for garnish

RECIPE FOLLOWS

Make the curry: In a large saucepan, melt the butter over medium-low heat. Add the onions and cook, stirring occasionally, adding the garlic and ginger after 10 minutes. Cook until the onions are deeply caramelized, 8 to 10 more minutes.

Add the fennel seeds, cardamom pods, coriander seeds, and cumin seeds; cook until they are aromatic, about 3 minutes. Stir in the tomato paste and cook until it is heated through, 1 to 2 minutes. Add the wine, turn up the heat slightly, and cook until it fully evaporates, about 3 minutes.

Add the cream and chicken stock and bring to a boil, then turn the heat down to a simmer and add the garam masala, curry powder, and cayenne. Simmer, partially covered, for 15 minutes.

Remove the cardamom pods, season the curry with the salt and lime juice, then puree the sauce in a blender or food processor until smooth. Set it aside and keep warm.

Make the rice: Rinse and drain the rice. In a medium saucepan, add the rice and 2¼ cups (540 ml) water; cover and bring it to a boil. Reduce the heat slightly and simmer the rice for 20 minutes. Turn off the heat and let the pot sit for 10 more minutes. Fluff the rice with a fork before serving.

While the rice cooks, season the fish fillets with salt and pepper. In a skillet large enough to hold the fillets without crowding them, heat grapeseed oil to cover the bottom of the pan over medium-high heat. When the oil shimmers, add the fillets to the pan skin side down.

Cook the fish until a nice crust forms on the skin, about 3 minutes, then flip the fillets over, reduce the heat, and add the butter. Baste the fish with the butter until it is cooked through, 2 to 3 minutes more.

Serve each fillet with warm curry sauce and black rice and garnish with fresh cilantro.

BARBECUED RIBS

WITH *charred escarole* AND *savory bread pudding*

SERVES 10 TO 12

The first summer after we reopened post-hurricane, I added ribs to our menu simply because I wanted to eat them. This recipe was really one of those "What do we have on hand?" type dishes. We'd already started playing around with a Korean *bibimbap* for brunch, so I had the gochujang that ended up in this barbecue sauce. Its sweet and spicy mellow flavors get a little zing from the Szechuan peppercorns in the rib rub. We had lots of Swiss chard and extra bread for bread pudding. So I chopped up the chard and folded it into a savory, complexly spiced bread pudding that complements the spicy sweetness of the ribs. Add some greens on the side and it's a proper plate of barbecue.

TIP *I always opt for Berkshire pork, because the breed is fatty and flavorful. Regular supermarket pork won't be the same, but you could use another heritage breed or try pork from an Asian market, which generally has more fat.*

FOR THE RIBS

2 tablespoons Szechuan peppercorns
2 tablespoons whole coriander seeds
1/4 cup (50 g) sugar
1/4 cup (36 g) kosher salt
2 racks St. Louis–cut or whole spareribs
1 cup (240 ml) cola
3 cups (720 ml) chicken stock

FOR THE BARBECUE SAUCE

1/3 cup (75 ml) ketchup
1/3 cup (75 ml) gochujang (Korean red chile paste; see page 21)
3 tablespoons molasses
1 tablespoon dark mushroom soy sauce
1 tablespoon rice wine vinegar

FOR THE ESCAROLE

1 head escarole, washed, dried, and leaves separated
2 tablespoons olive oil
Juice of 1/2 lemon (about 1 1/2 tablespoons)
Kosher salt and freshly ground black pepper
Savory Bread Pudding (recipe follows)

The day before you plan to serve the dish, prepare the ribs: In a hot dry pan, toast the peppercorns and coriander seeds over medium-high heat, stirring occasionally, and then grind them very finely or crush them in a zip-top bag with a rolling pin.

Rub the spices, sugar, and salt all over the ribs, wrap them well in plastic wrap, and refrigerate them overnight.

The next day, preheat the oven to 325°F (165°C). Place the ribs in a baking dish with the cola and chicken stock, then cover tightly and braise until very tender, 2 to 2 1/2 hours.

Meanwhile, make the barbecue sauce: In a small bowl, whisk together the ketchup, gochujang, molasses, soy sauce, and rice vinegar. Set aside.

Heat a gas or charcoal grill to high heat. (You can also finish the dish on a stovetop griddle or grill pan, or use your broiler.)

Toss the escarole leaves with the olive oil and set aside.

RECIPE CONTINUES

Grill the ribs until they are marked on each side, 2 to 3 minutes per side. Brush them with some of the barbecue sauce and grill for 30 seconds more on each side, or until they are nicely marked and the sauce is sticky. Set aside.

Grill the escarole leaves until wilted and slightly charred, about 30 seconds per side. In a medium bowl, toss the leaves with the lemon juice and season to taste with salt and pepper.

Cut apart the ribs and serve them with the grilled escarole, a wedge of savory bread pudding, and the remaining barbecue sauce.

SAVORY BREAD PUDDING

SERVES 10 TO 12

You can prepare this up to a day in advance, then bake it the day you serve it. If you want it to be warm when you serve it, bake it after the ribs have come out of the oven and then grill them once the bread pudding is done. You can use any good-quality bread for this recipe.

8	ounces (225 g) thick-cut bacon (about 5 slices), cut into ½-inch (12-mm) dice
1	small onion, diced
1	bunch Swiss chard, stems thinly sliced and leaves separated, and roughly chopped
6	large eggs
1½	cups (360 ml) heavy cream
1½	cups (360 ml) chicken stock
1	teaspoon cayenne pepper
¼	teaspoon ground cinnamon
	Pinch ground cloves
1	teaspoon kosher salt
10	cups (400 g) 1-inch (2.5-cm) cubes bread, such as French, sourdough, wheat, or rye Unsalted butter, for greasing the pan
2	cups (8 ounces/225 g) grated Gruyère cheese
½	cup (50 g) grated Parmigiano-Reggiano cheese

In a large skillet, cook the bacon over medium-high heat until crisp, about 7 minutes. Remove it from the pan with a slotted spoon and let it drain on paper towels. Pour off most of the bacon fat and reserve it, leaving just a skim of grease on the pan.

In the same pan, sauté the onion and chard stems over medium-high heat until they are tender and the onion is slightly colored, about 5 minutes. Fold the leaves in, cooking just until they wilt, 1 to 2 minutes. Turn off the heat and set them aside.

In a large bowl, whisk together the eggs, cream, chicken stock, cayenne, cinnamon, cloves, and salt. Fold in the bread and stir until the cubes are thoroughly moistened. Let stand at least 1 hour, or cover tightly and refrigerate up to overnight.

Preheat the oven to 350°F (175°C) and grease a large rectangular baking dish with butter.

Fold the chard, bacon, and both cheeses into the soaked bread. Transfer the bread pudding in the greased baking dish, cover loosely with foil, and bake for 20 minutes.

Uncover and bake for another 20 minutes, until the top is slightly crusty and browned and the bread pudding is slightly springy to the touch, not wet. Serve it warm or at room temperature.

PORK CHOPS

WITH *creamy leeks, spaetzle,* AND *guajillo sauce*

SERVES 4

Do pork chops, creamy leeks, and späetzle—a rustic Germanic egg noodle or little dumpling—even need a sauce? No, but the one we added puts it over the top. It's our sous chef Rigo's: Adding chiles to things is a no-brainer for him, given his Mexican heritage. Over the years he picked up lots of culinary school tricks in our kitchen, like creating a symphony of flavors with disparate elements of a dish and paying attention to them at every step. A little here and there, and the whole thing makes sense. My contribution? The leeks and the spaetzle.

TIP *To serve this dish for a party, make the leeks, sauce, and spaetzle a day ahead.*

FOR THE GUAJILLO SAUCE

- 2 dried guajillo chiles
- 1 dried chile de arbol
- 1 cup (240 ml) chicken stock
- 1 plum tomato
- 2 tablespoons Dijon mustard
- 1 clove garlic
- 1/4 teaspoon ground cumin
- 1 cup (240 ml) fresh blood orange juice, or use equal parts cranberry and orange juice
- 2 tablespoons sugar
- 3 tablespoons cold unsalted butter, cut into small pieces

FOR THE SPAETZLE

- 3 cups (375 g) all-purpose flour
- 1 tablespoon kosher salt
  Pinch nutmeg
- 4 large eggs
- 1 1/4 to 1 1/2 cups (300 to 360 ml) whole milk
  Olive oil
- 3 tablespoons unsalted butter

FOR THE LEEKS

- 2 tablespoons unsalted butter
- 1 small shallot, cut in to 1/4-inch (6-mm) dice
- 1 clove garlic
- 2 large leeks, white and light green parts thinly sliced
- 3/4 cup (180 ml) heavy cream
  Kosher salt and freshly ground black pepper

FOR THE PORK CHOPS

  Olive oil
- 4 (1 1/2-inch/4-cm thick) bone-in pork chops, patted dry
  Kosher salt and freshly ground black pepper

RECIPE FOLLOWS

Make the sauce: Seed and stem the dried chiles. Soak them in warm water until soft, about 1 hour. In a food processor or blender, puree the chiles with the chicken stock, tomato, mustard, garlic, and cumin and set aside.

In a medium saucepan, bring the orange juice and sugar to a simmer and reduce by half, about 15 minutes. Add the guajillo puree and simmer until reduced to a sauce-like consistency, 15 to 20 minutes more. Set aside.

Make the spaetzle: In a mixing bowl, combine the flour, salt, and nutmeg. In another large mixing bowl, whisk together the eggs and 1¼ cups (300 ml) of the milk. Whisk the dry ingredients into the milk, adding more milk if necessary to create what looks like a thick pancake batter. Bring a large pot of water to a boil and line a baking sheet with parchment paper.

Using a pastry bag (or a grater, colander, potato ricer, or spaetzle maker), press small pieces of the dough into the boiling water, a few at a time. They cook very fast—about 1 minute. When they float, they're done. Remove them from the pot with a strainer or slotted spoon, shake off the extra water, and place them on the baking sheet.

When all the spaetzle are cooked and cool, dress them with a little olive oil on the baking sheet so they don't stick together and set them aside. (Cover and refrigerate the baking sheet if not serving in the next hour.)

Make the leeks: In a skillet over medium heat, melt the butter. Cook the shallot and garlic for 1 minute, then add the leeks and cook for 3 minutes more. Add the heavy cream and reduce it over medium-low heat until it is creamy and not soupy, about 10 minutes, then season it with salt and pepper. Set aside.

Make the pork chops: In a large skillet, add just enough oil to coat the pan and heat it over medium-high heat. Season the dry chops with salt and pepper, then cook them in batches for 3 to 4 minutes per side for medium, or still slightly pink inside. Set them aside, and when all four chops are cooked, wipe the pan clean and add the 3 tablespoons butter for the spaetzle.

Add the spaetzle, and cook them in the butter over medium-high heat until they are browned and a little crispy. Stir in the creamy leeks until they are heated through, then taste for salt and pepper.

Reheat the guajillo sauce, whisk in the 3 tablespoons cold butter for the sauce, then serve each pork chop with some spaetzle and leeks, topping both with warm sauce.

BRAISED BERKSHIRE PORK BELLY

WITH *cranberry bean salad* AND *arugula–walnut pesto*

SERVES 4 TO 6

When we created this dish, everybody was braising pork belly. For me it was natural, because in South Korea they currently love pork belly. They call it "three layers of skin," because there are often three layers of meat and three layers of fat. There's a hint of sweetness to the braise for the pork, and the chunky pesto adds the right amount of bitterness to really make this dish. You don't have to strain and reduce the braising liquid—after you remove the belly, but that's what we always do at the restaurant with any braising liquid—and then we add it to the dish. We call it our magic sauce.

> **TIP** *You don't have to roast the garlic cloves for the pesto, but raw garlic can be so intense—that step really smooths them out. I toss them with olive oil, salt, and pepper and roast them until tender. The ideal time to do this is when you have the oven on while you are braising the pork. Ideally, you'll also soak the beans and brine the pork overnight the day before you want to make this dish.*

FOR THE CRANBERRY BEAN SALAD

8	ounces (225 g) dried cranberry beans
1	medium shallot, thinly sliced
2	cloves garlic, minced
3	tablespoons red wine vinegar
1/4	cup (60 ml) olive oil
1	tablespoon Dijon mustard
1	teaspoon kosher salt

FOR THE BRINE

1/2	cup (135 g) kosher salt
2	tablespoons granulated sugar
2	teaspoons coriander seeds
1	teaspoon fennel seeds
1	teaspoon dried juniper berries
1	bay leaf
2	sprigs fresh thyme
1	handful parsley stems (optional)
3-	to 4-pound (1.4- to 1.8-kg) piece of pork belly

FOR THE BRAISE

	Kosher salt and freshly ground black pepper
1	medium onion, diced
1	medium carrot, diced
1	leek, white part only, cleaned and roughly chopped
5	cloves garlic, smashed with the side of a knife
2	sprigs fresh thyme
2	cups (480 ml) white wine
3/4	cup (180 ml) apple cider vinegar
1/4	cup (55 g) packed brown sugar
4	to 6 cups (960 ml to 1.4 L) chicken stock
2	tablespoons cold unsalted butter

FOR THE ARUGULA-WALNUT PESTO

4	packed cups (160 g) baby arugula
1/2	cup (120 ml) extra-virgin olive oil, plus extra as needed
1/2	cup (50 g) walnuts, lightly roasted
6	cloves roasted garlic (see Tip)
	Juice from 1/2 lemon (about 1 1/2 tablespoons)
	Kosher salt

RECIPE FOLLOWS

The night before you want to make this dish, soak the beans: Cover them with several inches of water and a pinch of salt and let them soak overnight.

At the same time, make the brine: In a large heavy pot, bring 5 cups (1.2 L) water to a boil with the salt, sugar, coriander seeds, fennel seeds, juniper berries, bay leaf, thyme, and parsley stems, if using. Let it cool completely.

Put the pork belly in a nonreactive container, and add the brine so the meat is submerged. Brine overnight, refrigerated (or for at least 4 hours).

Make the braise: Preheat the oven to 300°F (150°C).

Remove the belly from the brine, rinse it off, and dry it well. Discard the brine. Salt and pepper all sides of the pork. Heat a Dutch oven or ovenproof pot over high heat and brown all sides (skin side first) of the pork. Remove the meat from the pot and set it aside.

Add the onion, carrot, and leek and cook over medium-high heat, stirring frequently, until they are soft and translucent. Add the garlic and thyme and continue to cook, stirring frequently, until the mixture browns slightly. Add the wine and vinegar and bring it to a simmer. Let it simmer—do not let it boil—until the mixture is reduced by half.

Stir in the brown sugar and chicken stock; add the belly and let it braise in the preheated oven until it is very tender but not totally falling apart, about 2 hours.

Meanwhile, make the bean salad: Bring a large saucepan of water to a boil and cook the drained beans until they are tender, about 30 to 45 minutes. Drain and let them cool, then dress them with the shallot, garlic, vinegar, oil, and mustard. Season with the salt and set aside.

Make the pesto: In a food processor or blender, puree the arugula, oil, walnuts, and garlic, adding more olive oil as necessary. Season with the lemon juice, starting with a tablespoon or so, and salt, then set aside.

When the belly is tender, remove the meat from the braising liquid and set it aside with a little bit of the liquid so that it doesn't dry out. Strain the braising liquid, bring it to a simmer, and swirl in the cold butter until it emulsifies and becomes a sauce.

To serve, cut the belly into 4 to 6 pieces. Place the beans in a deep bowl topped with a serving of pork belly, then top with the sauce and a dollop of pesto.

PASTA

WITH *oxtail* IN *miso cream*

SERVES 6 TO 8

Even though fresh pasta is a serious, labor-intensive dish for a small kitchen like ours, we always have one on the menu. This one, made with fresh tagliatelle, earned raves, and it was dreamed up by our head chef Sam in the dead of winter, when he wanted a thick, hearty sauce that would warm you up from the inside out. It's Chef Sam at his best, thinking outside of the pasta box. It is a truly unctuous concoction of silky oxtail meat with bar-none flavor, thanks to the addition of miso, chile, and a heavy dose of cream. Let's just say it's not low-calorie.

3	pounds (1.4 kg) oxtails, cut into 2-inch (5-cm)-thick rounds
	Kosher salt
4	tablespoons (60 ml) canola oil
¼	cup (60 ml) shiro (white) miso
¾	cup (180 ml) heavy cream
1	large onion, finely diced
1	jalapeño, seeded, stemmed, and minced
3	cloves garlic, minced
2	tablespoons fresh marjoram leaves, plus extra for garnish
½	cup (50 g) freshly grated Parmigiano-Reggiano or Pecorino Romano cheese, plus extra for garnish
1	pound (455 g) dried spaghetti, or ½ recipe pasta dough from page 47 cut for spaghetti
	Juice from ½ lemon (about 1 ½ tablespoons)

Preheat the oven to 450°F (230°C).

Place the oxtails on a rimmed baking sheet; dust them liberally with salt and toss with 2 tablesoons of the canola oil. Roast them, turning them from time to time, until well-browned all over, about 25 minutes. Reduce the oven to 350°F (175°C).

Transfer the oxtails to a Dutch oven. Cover them with water by 1 inch (2.5 cm) and braise them in the oven for 3 hours, or until they are falling off the bone. Let them cool in the liquid, then pick the meat from the bones and set it aside, covered with enough stock to keep the meat from drying out.

Meanwhile, in a small saucepan, whisk together the miso and cream and lightly warm them over low heat. Scrape the miso cream into a large serving bowl.

Heat the remaining 2 tablespoons oil in a large skillet over low heat and cook the onion, jalapeño, and garlic until dry and slightly browned, about 30 minutes. Add them to the miso cream in the serving bowl.

Add the marjoram leaves, grated cheese, and picked oxtail meat to the cream and set aside while you make the pasta.

Cook the pasta in boiling salted water until al dente, reserving 1 cup (240 ml) of the cooking liquid. Put the hot pasta into the serving bowl and toss it with the miso cream, vegetables, and oxtail meat until all the strands are nicely coated, adding pasta water if necessary to make a sauce-like consistency. Taste for seasoning, add the lemon juice, and toss again.

Serve immediately, sprinkled with more marjoram and cheese.

WILD BOAR SHANKS

WITH *apple pickles* AND *bacon*

SERVES 6

I love braises, and for our reopening menu after Hurricane Sandy, I wanted to do something interesting. Here, the apple pickles add just a touch of something sweet. It's actually a riff on Korean short ribs, which are cooked with dates. This is just another way to use fruit for sweetness. Once we add the grits—which we often use as a platform for meats instead of polenta—the dish is a cool twist on the classic American corn, pig, and apple trio.

> **TIP** *As I discuss on page xx, I like to soak my grits for a few hours or overnight. It cuts the cooking time considerably.*

FOR THE GRITS

2	cups (240 g) stone-ground coarse grits
½	cup (120 ml) whole milk
3	tablespoons unsalted butter, or more, to taste
¼	cup (25 g) freshly grated Parmigiano-Reggiano cheese
	Kosher salt and freshly ground black pepper

FOR THE APPLE PICKLES

2	cups (360 g) diced Granny Smith apples
½	cup (120 ml) apple cider vinegar
3	tablespoons sugar
2	tablespoons kosher salt
1	tablespoon minced shallots
¼	teaspoon crushed red pepper flakes
1	bay leaf

FOR THE BRAISE

8	ounces (225 g) slab bacon, cut into 2-inch (5-cm) cubes
6	wild boar shanks (about 5 pounds/2.3 kg)
	Kosher salt and freshly ground black pepper
1	medium onion, finely diced
1	medium carrot, finely diced
1	leek, white part only, finely chopped
1	large Granny Smith apple, peeled
2	teaspoons fennel seeds, toasted and ground
2	teaspoons coriander seeds, toasted and ground
1 ½	cups (360 ml) white wine
1 ½	cups (360 ml) red wine
¾	cup (180 ml) white balsamic vinegar
3	bay leaves
2	quarts (2 L) chicken stock
	Chopped chives or scallions, for garnish

Prep the grits: In a large heavy-bottomed pot, soak the grits in 2 quarts (2 L) water for a few hours or overnight.

Make the pickles: Put the apples in a heatproof bowl. In a medium pot, bring the vinegar, sugar, salt, shallots, chile flakes, and bay leaf to a boil. Pour the pickling liquid over the apples and set aside.

Make the braise: Preheat the oven to 325°F (165°C).

In a Dutch oven, brown the bacon on all sides over medium-high heat, 5 to 7 minutes. Remove the bacon from the pan, leaving the bacon fat in the pan.

Sprinkle the shanks with salt and pepper. Brown the shanks in the bacon fat, about 8 minutes per batch, and set them aside. In the same pan, brown the onion, carrot, leek, and apple, then stir in the toasted and ground fennel and coriander seeds.

Add both wines, the vinegar, and bay leaves and cook for 5 to 10 minutes, until it reduces slightly.

Add the stock and bring the liquid to a boil. Add the shanks, making sure they are covered in the liquid; cover the pot and braise the shanks in the oven for 3½ hours, or until they are tender, adding the bacon back to the pot after 2 hours.

While the shanks cook, make the grits: In the soaking pot, bring the grits to a simmer in their soaking water and cook, stirring constantly, until they are tender, about 15 minutes. Stir in the milk, butter, and cheese and season with salt and pepper. Set aside and keep warm.

When the shanks are tender, remove them from the sauce. Strain it and bring it to a simmer over medium-high heat, cooking until the sauce reduces slightly.

Serve the grits in deep bowls topped with the shanks and pieces of bacon. Top them both with sauce and the pickled apples. Garnish with chopped chives or scallions.

PORK SHOYU RAMEN

SERVES 8

When our neighborhood was struggling after Hurricane Sandy, I decided to put ramen on the menu to get people down to Red Hook. Ramen wasn't as easy to find back then, but diners were already crazy for it, and it was a cold winter. What happened instead was that it lured the locals, who were looking for something different in the 'hood. Now we call ramen night "community night." It takes some time to make the broth—it's a two-day project—but it is well worth it.

> **TIP** *You can use any ramen noodles, dried or fresh, but this would also work with somen noodles or even regular dried pasta in a pinch. We get our fresh ramen from Sun Noodle.*

FOR THE BROTH

- 1 pig trotter
- 2 tablespoons canola or grapeseed oil
- 1 small onion, skin on and quartered
- 1 medium carrot, cut into large chunks
- 1 (2-inch/5-cm) piece fresh ginger
- 1 tablespoon tomato paste
- 1 head garlic, cloves peeled and bundled in cheesecloth
- 1 bunch scallions
- 1 pound (455 g) chicken wings
- ½ rack spareribs (4 to 5 ribs)
- 1 handful dried shiitake mushrooms
- 2 teaspoons kosher salt

FOR THE ROAST PORK BUTT

- 1 tablespoon sugar
- 1 tablespoon kosher salt
- 1 pork butt (3 to 4 pounds/1.4 to 1.8 kg)

FOR THE *MENMA* (BAMBOO SHOOTS)

- 8 ounces (225 g) canned bamboo shoots, drained
- 3 tablespoons soy sauce
- ¼ cup (60 ml) mirin
- 2 tablespoons sake
- 1 tablespoon plus 1 teaspoon sugar

FOR THE *TARE* (SEASONING)

- ⅓ cup (75 ml) soy sauce
- ¼ cup (60 ml) mirin
- ¼ cup (60 ml) sake

FOR THE FINISHED DISH

- 4 large eggs
- 1 pound (455 g) fresh ramen or Chinese wheat noodles
- 8 heads baby bok choy, blanched
- ½ bunch scallions, sliced on the bias

RECIPE FOLLOWS

The day before you plan to serve the ramen, blanch the trotter: Place the trotter in a large pot with water to cover, bring it to a boil, then turn off the heat and pour off the water.

Meanwhile, in a 10- to 12-quart (9.6- to 11.4-L) stockpot, heat the oil over medium-low heat and cook the onion, carrot, and ginger until the onion is translucent. Add the tomato paste and cook for another 3 minutes. Add the bundled garlic and the scallions, then the blanched trotter, wings, spareribs, and mushrooms, along with 8 quarts (7.5 L) water and the salt. Cover and bring to a boil. Adjust the heat to cook at a brisk simmer, loosely covered, for 6 hours.

Cool, then strain out the solids and remove the garlic from the cheesecloth. In a blender, puree the garlic with a little broth, then add this back to the rest of the broth for extra body and flavor. Cool and refrigerate the broth.

Make the pork butt: Preheat the oven to 300°F (150°C).

Mix the sugar and salt, and rub it all over the meat. Roast for 3 hours, or until the internal temperature is 180 to 190°F (82 to 88°C) and the cartilage and fat has melted. Let it cool and then refrigerate it.

MISO RAMEN

SERVES 8

You remember that trick with the pureed garlic and fermented beans I used to add oomph to the Roast Chicken with Chinese Black Bean Sauce (page 97)? I also used that here to make a vegan ramen broth with tons of depth and flavor. You won't miss the protein. You get all the umami you need from the dried mushrooms, the kelp, the vegetables, and that garlic. You can also make the entire dish vegan if you leave out the eggs.

FOR THE BROTH

3	tablespoons canola oil
2	large onions, peeled and quartered
3	large carrots, roughly chopped
1	(2-inch/5-cm) piece fresh ginger
2	tablespoons black peppercorns
3	tablespoons tomato paste
2	cups (70 g) dried shiitake mushrooms
1	(8-inch/13-g) square piece kombu seaweed
1	bunch scallions, cut into thirds
2	heads garlic, cloves peeled and bundled in cheesecloth
1	tablespoon kosher salt
3/4	cup (180 ml) shiro (white) miso

FOR THE *MENMA* (BAMBOO SHOOTS)

8	ounces (225 g) canned bamboo shoots, drained
3	tablespoons soy sauce
1/4	cup (60 ml) mirin
2	tablespoons sake
1	tablespoon plus 1 teaspoon sugar

FOR THE FINISHED DISH

4	large eggs (optional)
1	pound (455 g) fresh ramen or Chinese wheat noodles
8	heads baby bok choy, blanched
2	sheets nori, cut into quarters
1/2	bunch scallions, sliced on the bias

Make the broth: In a large stockpot, heat the canola oil over medium-high heat and cook the onions, carrots, and ginger until lightly browned, about 5 minutes.

Lower the heat to medium, add the peppercorns and tomato paste, and cook for 5 minutes more.

Add 5 quarts (4.7 L) water and the mushrooms, seaweed, scallions, bundled garlic, and salt. Bring them to a boil, then simmer for 2 hours.

Meanwhile, make the menma: In a small saucepan, combine the bamboo shoots, soy sauce, mirin, sake, and sugar. Bring them to a simmer and cook for 10 minutes, or until the sauce is thick and syrupy. Set aside.

Cook the eggs, if using, by bringing a pot of water to a boil and preparing a pot or bowl of ice-cold water. Gently lower the eggs in the boiling water, reduce the heat to a low simmer, and cook them for 7 minutes. Shock them in cold water. Peel them, cut them in half, and set them aside.

Cook the noodles: Briefly blanch fresh noodles in a large pot of boiling water and set them aside, or cook dried pasta according to the package directions.

When the broth is done, strain it and remove the garlic from the cheesecloth. In a blender, puree the garlic with a little broth and the miso. Return it to the pot and keep the broth hot.

To compose the ramen, add 1½ cups (360 ml) hot broth to each bowl. Add the noodles, bok choy, seaweed, scallions, and menma, and top with a soft-boiled egg half, if using. Serve immediately.

CHAPTER FIVE

Son Mat and Insa

IN RECENT YEARS, I DECLARED SUNDAY TO BE FAMILY DAY, spent with Ben and our kids. The kitchen at The Good Fork was solid, and I didn't need to be on call all the time. Most chefs try to go out to eat to try all different kinds of restaurants on their days off, but lately Ben and I just wanted to eat Korean food. So we'd pile in the car and drive all the way out to Flushing, a New York City neighborhood in the borough of Queens filled with Korean markets, restaurants, and businesses, to eat grilled kalbi and *soondae* (Korean blood sausage) or big bowls of *soondubu*, a spicy Korean tofu stew.

I was making Korean standards even more often at home, too: It's what I craved. That is why for our second restaurant, Ben and I knew we wanted it to be classically Korean in concept. Over the years, I've grown to realize what it is I find so appealing about the food I grew up with. It is very much like Italian food: The Korean pantry, like the Italian one, is not huge. We use just a handful of ingredients—rice, anchovies, seaweed, seasonal vegetables, and pantry items—but we combine them in so many ways, changing up the proportions or combinations. As a home cook or a chef, the limitations are somehow exciting.

Also like Italian food, Korean food is highly seasonal—you use what is available at a given time of year. I've mentioned it before—when I was growing up in Korea, most families did not eat a lot of meat, so we rarely had the barbecue that most Americans consider to be Korean food. We ate vegetables and fish and seaweeds and soups, and we kimcheed vegetables slowly over the cold months. Which is why even though our new restaurant (called Insa, meaning "to greet") is a barbecue spot, I kept a strong focus on seasonal vegetables, fish, and soups. I also put as much effort into my *banchan*—those delectable small plates of pickled vegetables, condiments, and sides that come with every Korean meal—as I do into my *bulgogi* marinade.

Many of the recipes in this chapter are from Insa. I consider them to be the greatest hits of basic Korean cooking—the dishes that should be in the American lexicon of great food. *Son mat* is a Korean term that means "taste of the hand," or something made by somebody with both passion and skill.

Please note that these are truly traditional recipes, so they occasionally require a trip to an Asian market. In many recipes in this book, I suggest substitutes for where you might use a non-Korean ingredient. Here, things just won't taste the same unless you're using the real deal as described on page 20.

BANCHAN FOR THE TABLE

EACH SERVES 4 TO 6 AS PART OF A LARGER MEAL

When we moved from Korea to the United States, my father went over some basic American dining ground rules with my siblings and me. You don't burp at the table—in Korea, burping at the table isn't rude, but a sign that you had a good meal—and you don't share your food. In America, my dad told us, everybody gets their own plate, and everything you are going to eat is on it. I remember being shocked: "There's no banchan?" *Banchan* [BAHN-chan] means "side dishes." At the Korean dinner table, everybody gets their own bowl of plain or Mixed Rice (page 191)—you don't share that—but we share all the other side dishes, which vary each season or according to what you happen to have on hand and usually include at least one kind of kimchee. We don't worry about

double-dipping. Banchan are always on the table, for every meal—they're really the heart of the meal. Sometimes a meal is just your rice and those side dishes, and you put a little of the latter on your rice. In fact, the general idea is you have a rice cooker keeping rice warm all day long, and then there's always banchan in the fridge, so you're ready to eat at any time. Most banchan are eaten cold or at room temperature.

TIP *Note that with these recipes, fresh is always best. These banchan will last in the fridge for only 2 or 3 days. The high water content of the vegetables makes them prone to spoilage. If you have any left-overs, eat them in the form of the bibimbap on page 208 with my spicy sauce and, of course, a fried egg!*

KOREAN POTATO SALAD
(*Gam Ja Jo Rim*)

There are fifty ways to do potatoes for banchan. I picked this one because it combines a typical Korean pan-sauté technique and a nice marinade.

8   large or 4 small (1 pound/450 g) Yukon gold potatoes
2   tablespoons mirin
2   tablespoons soy sauce
2   tablespoons rice wine vinegar
2   teaspoons sugar
2   teaspoons gochujaru (Korean dried red pepper flakes; see page 21)
1   to 2 tablespoons olive oil
2   teaspoons sesame oil

Cut the potatoes into 2 by ¼-inch (5-cm by 6-mm) matchstick strips, then rinse them off to

remove any extra starch, and set them aside in a colander to drain.

In a small bowl, whisk together the mirin, soy sauce, vinegar, sugar, and gochujaru. This is your dressing.

In a large skillet, heat the olive oil over medium heat and cook the potatoes, stirring them as you do, for 1 minute. Pour in ½ cup (120 ml) water and cook until all the water evaporates. Add the dressing to the pan and keep stirring and cooking the potatoes. After about 5 minutes—before they are cooked through—add the sesame oil and continue stirring and cooking until the potatoes still have a little bite but are not mushy, 2 to 5 minutes more. You might need to add a little water if the pan is very dry. Serve hot, warm, or at room temperature.

EGGPLANT
(*Gaji Muchim*)

This is a simple banchan technique. You take a seasonal vegetable and steam it, then dress it with this marinade. You can do this with summer or winter squash or beans.

1   pound (455 g) Asian eggplants, halved lengthwise and cut into thirds
1   scallion, sliced
2   cloves garlic, minced
2   tablespoons soy sauce
2   teaspoons sesame oil
1   teaspoon myeol chi aek jeot (Korean anchovy fish sauce; see page 21) or fish sauce
1   teaspoon gochujaru (Korean dried red pepper flakes; see page 21)
½   teaspoon sugar or rice syrup (optional) Kosher salt

In a pot over simmering water, steam the eggplants until very soft and cooked through, 3 to 5 minutes. Let them cool slightly, then use your fingers to pull apart the eggplants into long bite-size pieces. In a mixing bowl, toss the eggplant with the scallion, garlic, soy sauce, sesame oil, fish sauce, gochujaru, and sugar, if using. Season to taste with kosher salt.

SOYBEAN SPROUT SALAD
(*Kong-Namul Muchim*)

This is a good recipe to use up any leftover seaweed from making dashi or stock. Otherwise, cook the kombu in a little bit of water until it is soft, about 15 minutes.

1   pound (455 g) soybean sprouts, trimmed
1   tablespoon soy sauce
1   tablespoon rice wine vinegar
1   tablespoon kosher salt
2   cloves garlic, minced
2   teaspoons sesame oil
1½   teaspoons sugar
1   teaspoon gochujaru (Korean dried red pepper flakes; see page xx)
1   teaspoon myeol chi aek jeot (Korean anchovy fish sauce; see page 21) or fish sauce (optional)
1   cup cooked kombu seaweed, cut into 2 by ¼-inch (5-cm by 6-mm) matchstick strips
1   scallion, minced
2   teaspoons sesame seeds

In a pot over simmering water, steam the sprouts until cooked through, 5 to 8 minutes.

In a large mixing bowl, whisk together the soy sauce, vinegar, salt, garlic, sesame oil, sugar, gochujaru, and fish sauce. Add the steamed sprouts and kombu, tossing to mix. Stir in the scallion and sesame seeds and taste for salt.

GREEN SQUASH STIR-FRY WITH SHRIMP PASTE
(*HoBak Bokkum*)

1 tablespoon grapeseed oil

½ large yellow onion, sliced

2 pounds (910 g) summer squash, sliced into ⅛-inch (3-mm)-thick half moons

1 tablespoon minced garlic

1 tablespoon shrimp paste or chopped anchovy

1 teaspoon kosher salt

¼ cup (60 ml) Master Korean Dashi (page 205)

2 cheong-gochu (Korean green chile peppers; see page 21) or shishitos, seeded, stemmed, and thinly sliced

1 tablespoon sesame oil

1 teaspoon sesame seeds

In a skillet, heat the grapeseed oil over medium heat. Cook the onion for 3 minutes, then add the squash, garlic, shrimp paste, and salt and cook for 2 minutes more.

Add the dashi, cover the pan, and cook for 3 minutes. Add the chile peppers and cook until they are tender, about 2 minutes more. Add the sesame oil and sesame seeds and toss to combine.

DRIED RADISH
(*Mumallaengi Muchim*)

You can find bags of Korean or Chinese dried radish, which is pieces of white radish that have been shredded or sliced and then sun-dried, in Asian grocery stores. The package will usually say "dried radish" in English. Their flavor is a concentrated blend of sweetness and umami that we enhance with the anchovy/shrimp paste, sugar, and a bit of hot chile.

2 cups (230 g) shredded or cut dried radish

3 tablespoons rice syrup

¼ cup gochujaru (Korean dried red pepper flakes; see page 21)

1 tablespoon chopped anchovy or shrimp paste

½ tablespoon minced garlic

1 teaspoon sugar

1 teaspoon sesame seeds

1 teaspoon sesame oil

1 tablespoon of thinly sliced scallions

Rehydrate dried radish in cold tap water for 10 minutes. Rinse a few times and drain well.

In a small bowl, mix together the radish, rice syrup, gochujaru, anchovy, garlic, sugar, sesame seeds, sesame oil, and scallions.

STEWED BEANS
(*Kongjang*)

Typically this dish came about as a way to preserve these beans for months at a time—so don't be afraid to keep them in the fridge for a few days. They are not soft but have a nice chewy texture.

1	pound (455 g) *sae-tae-ri* (dried black soy beans), soaked for 1 hour and drained
1	cup (240 ml) soy sauce
³⁄₄	cup (120 ml) mirin
³⁄₄	cup (120 ml) rice wine vinegar
¹⁄₃	cup (65 g) plus 2 tablespoons sugar

In a large saucepan, add fresh water to cover the soaked beans and bring them to a boil. Skim any solids that rise to the top and lower the heat. Add the soy sauce, mirin, vinegar, and ¹⁄₃ cup (65 g) of the sugar. Simmer for 1 hour, or until the beans are tender but not mushy. Finish by stirring in the remaining 2 tablespoons sugar.

SOY-BRAISED BEEF
(*Jangjorim*)

This is a great recipe not just for steak, but for any scraps of beef. The sauce is delicious on everything—the flavors of the meat and chiles and soy. Just pour it over rice and that's all you need.

1	pound (455 g) hanger steak, cut into 2-inch (5-cm) chunks
¹⁄₄	cup (35 g) diced onion
2	scallions, white and green parts, chopped
1	piece (3 ounces/85 g) daikon radish
11	cloves garlic, peeled
¹⁄₂	ounce peeled fresh ginger, sliced
¹⁄₂	teaspoon black peppercorns
3	tablespoons soy sauce
1 ¹⁄₂	tablespoons sugar
1 ¹⁄₂	tablespoons rice wine vinegar
4	or 5 cheong-gochu (Korean green chile peppers; see page 21) or jalapeños, cut into ¹⁄₂-inch (12-mm) slices
1	(3-inch/7.5-cm) piece kombu seaweed

In a large pot, combine the beef, onion, scallions, radish, 4 cloves of the garlic, the ginger, peppercorns, and 4 cups (960 ml) water. Cook, partially covered, over low heat for 30 minutes.

Remove the beef chunks and 1 cup (240 ml) of the cooking liquid and place them in a heavy-bottomed pot. Add the soy sauce, sugar, and vinegar and bring to a simmer for 10 minutes. Add the chiles, the remaining 7 cloves garlic, and the seaweed and cook until the liquid reduces and becomes syrupy, about 10 minutes.

MIXED RICE
(*Jap Gok Bap*)

In Korea, they also make this with mung beans, amaranth, black rice, black-eyed peas, sorghum, millet, buckwheat, kidney beans, cowpeas, sweet rice, or barley. In Korean markets, you will often see a bag of mixed grains called *jap gok*. The key is to soak the grains in advance; I also use French lentils here so they do not disintegrate. You don't add salt, because the rest of the banchan provides it. You could also serve plain white rice, as well. Note that unlike the rest of the banchan dishes, which are served communally, everyone gets their own bowl of rice.

1 cup (190 g) dry brown rice
1 cup (205 g) dry short-grain (sushi) rice
½ cup (100 g) lentils du Puy
½ cup (98 g) dried split green peas

In a medium saucepan, combine both rices, the lentils, and peas with 1 quart (960 ml) water and let them soak for 1 hour.

Bring to a boil, cover, and then reduce the heat to a low simmer. Cook until the peas and lentils are tender, about 25 minutes. Serve hot in individual bowls.

KIMCHEE

MAKES 1 GALLON (3.8 L)

Ask any Korean who makes kimchee about their recipe, and they will likely tell you they do something a little different from what you see here. They might use widely differing quantities of red pepper, garlic, and ginger, or skip the glutinous rice slurry. Or maybe they'll add all manner of fermented seafood or cut their vegetables to a different specific thickness. But this is my way—and in fact, there is no wrong way, as long as your fermentation is successful. The key is that it tastes good to you. That is why the most important thing when making kimchee is to taste your marinade before you add it to the cabbage, adding salt or ginger and so on as you like. Growing up in Korea, my mother and her friends would make kimchee together each fall—the way many Korean communities still do today—and gather around the tub on the ground taking tastes, adding more of this or a little of that, until it met everyone's expectations. That's why the amount of chiles here is a range, so you can adjust it to be as spicy as you'd like. Speaking of chiles, it's a good idea to invest in a box of disposable plastic gloves if you plan to make kimchee often, as the marinade can stain your hands. Note that the fish sauce/oysters/salted shrimp are optional, if you want to make this vegan, but to me they are really necessary for the right flavor.

> **TIP** *You may choose to roughly chop the onions, red bell pepper, garlic, and ginger, then put them in a food processor and pulse until incorporated, then drain them in a colander to remove the excess water.*

FOR THE **CABBAGE**

2   large Napa cabbages (roughly 5 pounds/ 2.3 kg total), quartered

1   quart (4 cups) kosher salt

FOR THE **SLURRY**

1   tablespoon glutinous rice flour

FOR THE **MARINADE**

2   pounds (910 g) daikon radish, shredded or cut into 2 by $1/4$-inch (5-cm by 6-mm) matchstick strips

1   large onion, minced or grated

1   medium red bell pepper or 2 Korean red chiles, grated

5   tablespoons minced garlic

3   tablespoons minced peeled fresh ginger

$3/4$ to 1 $1/4$ cups gochujaru (Korean dried red pepper flakes; see page 21)

1   bunch scallions, white and green parts thinly sliced

$1/4$ cup (100 g) salted shrimp, (75 ml) myeol chi aek jeot (Korean anchovy fish sauce; see page 21) or fish sauce, or $11/2$ ounces (36 g) dried kombu seaweed (for vegetarian option only)

RECIPE FOLLOWS

Make the cabbage: Fill a large bowl or pot or your sink with 2 quarts (2 L) water and ¾ cup (112 g) of the salt, whisking to dissolve the salt. Dunk the cabbage quarters in the salted water, making sure all the leaves are rinsed.

Shake off any excess water and sprinkle a good amount of salt in the folds of all the leaves, using at least ¼ cup (35 g) or more salt per head.

Place the salted cabbage quarters in an empty large bowl or container and top with a weight, such as a large dinner plate topped with a brick wrapped in foil or a cast-iron pot. Overtime, the cabbage will release lots of water and its important that the cabbage be kept submerged in the salted brine. Let them sit for at least 6 hours, or until the leaves are so flexible you can fold them in half without breaking them. (The Korean term for this is *juginda*, which roughly translated means "to kill.")

Rinse the cabbage in three or four changes of water to clean off all the extra salt, then let the cabbage drain in a colander for 1 hour.

Meanwhile, make the slurry: In a small saucepan, bring 1 cup (240 ml) water to a boil and whisk in the rice flour. Cook over low heat until a thick paste forms, 5 to 7 minutes. Let cool.

Make the marinade: In your largest mixing bowl, combine the radish, onion, bell pepper, garlic, ginger, gochujaru, scallions, and salted shrimp, if using. Drain off any water from the vegetables that may have accumulated. (Water is an enemy of successful fermentation, so you want to get rid of it where you can.) Add the cooled slurry and mix together well—with your hands is really the best way. Taste the mix on a bit of the salted cabbage, adding more chiles, salt, or ginger, etc., to the marinade as you like.

Slather the marinade all over the cabbage quarters by placing a small amount on each leaf where it meets the stem, then smearing it up the leaf with your hands. Slather on more as needed until the whole vegetable is nicely bathed in the marinade.

Make a tight bundle with each piece of cabbage, and place them as you go in a large glass container or recycled, cleaned pickle or condiment jars, making sure there's at least 2 inches (5 cm) of space at the top for the bubbling action of the ongoing fermentation. (Note that it can be messy to pull out whole cabbage leaves from jars to use them later on, so some people prefer to cut the cabbages into smaller pieces at this point. This is called *gutjori* kimchee.)

Once they are filled, cover the jars tightly and keep them out on the counter for at least 24 hours and up to 2 days, then refrigerate. You can eat it right away or wait for a little more funk to kick in. At the restaurant, our kimchee is fermented in the fridge for 2 weeks or longer, but at home I let it go much longer. It will last for a very, very long time, though the taste and color changes over time as the fermentation process continues.

KIMCHEE IN 5 STEPS

STEP 1.

Salt and rinse the cabbages. Let them sit for at least 6 hours, or until the leaves are so flexible you can fold them in half without breaking them.

STEP 2.

Mix the marinade and slurry together well—with your hands is really the best way—and then taste the mix on a bit of the salted cabbage, adding salt or ginger, etc., as you like.

STEP 3.

Rub the marinade into the cabbages. I place a small amount on each leaf where it meets the stem, and then smear it up the leaf with my hands, slathering on more as needed until the whole plant is nicely bathed in the marinade.

STEP 4.

Pack the kimchee into nonreactive containers to ferment. Keep them out for 24 hours to 2 days on the counter, and then refrigerate.

STEP 5.

You can eat the kimchee right away or, if you prefer stronger flavor, let it ferment in the fridge for 2 weeks or longer.

SCALLION PANCAKES

WITH *seafood*
(*Haemul Pajun*)

SERVES 4 AS AN APPETIZER

Savory pancakes are very popular in Korea, and you can find all kinds of ingredients in them. My personal favorite is with shrimp, squid, and lots and lots of scallions and chile peppers. *Haemul* [hay MUL] means "seafood," and *pajun* [pah JUN] is "scallion pancakes." A nicely balanced dipping sauce is key! Eat them while fresh and still crisp around the edges.

FOR THE **DIPPING SAUCE**

- 1   scallion, white and green parts thinly sliced
- 2   tablespoons soy sauce
- 1   tablespoon rice wine vinegar
- 1   teaspoon sugar
- ½   teaspoon gochujaru (Korean dried red pepper flakes; see page 21)
- 1   teaspoon sesame oil
- 1   teaspoon sesame seeds

FOR THE **SCALLION PANCAKES**

- ½   cup (75 g) potato starch
- ½   cup (75 g) all-purpose flour
- 1   teaspoon kosher salt
- ½   teaspoon baking powder
- 1   cup (240 ml) ice-cold water or seltzer
- 1   cup (242 g) chopped fresh large shrimp
- 1   cup (217 g) thinly sliced squid rings
- 2   scallions, white and green parts, thinly sliced
- 1   cheong-gochu (Korean green chile pepper; see page 21) or shishito pepper, stemmed, seeded, and sliced
- 2   tablespoons vegetable oil

Make the dipping sauce: In a small bowl, whisk together the scallion, soy sauce, vinegar, sugar, gochujaru, sesame oil, and sesame seeds and set aside.

Make the pancakes: In a large bowl, mix the potato starch, flour, salt, and baking powder with the water until just combined. Fold in the shrimp, squid, scallions, and chile. Let the mixture sit while you prepare the hot pan.

In an 8- to 10-inch (20- to 25-cm) skillet, heat the vegetable oil over medium-high heat. Put half of the batter in the pan and spread it out evenly. Cook the pancake until it is browned and crisp around the edges, about 5 minutes per side. Cut it into eight pieces and serve it immediately with the dipping sauce. Repeat with the remaining batter to make a second pancake.

MUNG BEAN PANCAKES

WITH *chiles* AND *kimchee*
(*Bindaetteok*)

SERVES 4 AS AN APPETIZER

These are very hip these days. They're gluten free, vegetarian, and very tasty. I get many a compliment on these tasty little Korean pancakes. Even from the non-vegetarians! But for me, the memories of these pancakes go way back to my dream-like memory of Korea as a young kid, where it is covered with beautiful valleys and mountains, rivers and streams. Hiking is a regular pastime there, and you have many entrepreneurs selling edible wares off the paths as you exit. I remember watching women freshly grind soaked mung beans with stone wheels, mixing them with chiles, kimchee, pork, and foraged herbs and frying them up right there in their makeshift stalls. Talk about the most satisfying street food!

TIP *The mung beans for* bindaetteok *are yellow because the beans are hulled before they are split. Like most beans, you could soak them overnight in the refrigerator. In Korea, there is also a version of this pancake made with unhulled mung beans, which are green. Those pancakes are known as* nokdujeon.

FOR THE PANCAKES

2	cups (390 g) split yellow mung beans
½	cup (50 g) glutinous rice flour
1⅓	cups (405 g) chopped kimchee (page 193) with juice
1	cup (55 g) chopped scallions
2	tablespoons cheong-gochu (Korean green chile pepper; see page 21) or shishito, seeded and thinly sliced
2	tablespoons Holland red chile, or red long hots, thinly sliced
1	tablespoon minced peeled fresh ginger
1	tablespoon minced garlic
	Kosher salt
	Vegetable oil, for frying

FOR THE DIPPING SAUCE

2	tablespoons soy sauce
2	tablespoons rice wine vinegar
2	teaspoons honey
1	teaspoon sesame seeds
¼	teaspoon gochujaru (Korean dried red pepper flakes; see page 21)

Prepare the split yellow mung beans and glutinous rice flour: Soak the beans in several inches of water and the rice flour in 1 cup (240 ml) water for at least 3 hours.

Make the dipping sauce: In a small bowl, mix together the soy sauce, rice vinegar, honey, sesame seeds, and gochujaru. Set aside.

Make the pancakes: Drain and rinse the soaked mung beans. Add them to a food processor along with the soaked rice flour and its soaking water, then process them until mostly smooth, but with a few chunks, so the pancakes have some texture.

Transfer the mung beans to a mixing bowl and stir in 2 cups (480 ml) water, the kimchee and juice, scallions, chiles, ginger, and garlic. Season to taste with salt.

In a 10-inch (25-cm) skillet, heat a thin film of oil over medium to medium-high heat. When it is shimmering, cook 3-inch (7.5-cm) pancakes in batches until brown and crisp on the bottom, adding more oil as necessary. Flip and cook them until the other sides are browned, another 3 to 4 minutes, adding more oil if necessary. Remove them to a plate and keep them warm while you cook the remaining pancakes. Serve the pancakes hot with the dipping sauce.

VEGETABLE FRITTERS
(*Yachae Twikim*)

SERVES 8 TO 10 AS AN APPETIZER

Twikim [TWEE-kyim] are one of Korea's foremost popular street snacks, sometimes made with shrimp or other fillings. These fritters are vegetable versions: *yachae* means "vegetable." You can substitute most any vegetable for these, but make sure you use one with low water content—no tomatoes. Tossing the vegetables in the dry flour mixture before you add the cold seltzer makes it easier to coat them in the batter. When you fry, be sure to drop the batter into the oil in a lacy form, which leads to more cracks and crevices. Those equal extra crispness.

> **TIP** *This dish is traditionally served with an herb called perilla or sesame leaves, which is the Korean version of shiso. They're both in the mint family, and the same way there are different kinds of basil, there are different types of shisho, which you'll find in shades of green to purple. Korean perilla has smoother edges and larger leaves. You can use the Japanese kind in a pinch, or any herb for that matter.*

Vegetable oil, for frying

2	cups (220 g) 2 by 1/4-inch (5-cm by 6-mm) matchstick strips carrot
2	cups (340 g) 2 by 1/4-inch (5-cm by 6-mm) matchstick strips sweet potato
1	cup (85 g) 2 by 1/4-inch (5-cm by 6-mm) matchstick strips zucchini
1/2	cup (85 g) 2 by 1/4-inch (5-cm by 6-mm) matchstick strips potato
1/2	cup (20 g) slivered fresh perilla or Japanese shiso
1	cup (125 g) plus 2 tablespoons all-purpose flour
1	cup (165 g) plus 2 tablespoons potato starch
1	teaspoon kosher salt, plus extra for sprinkling Ice-cold seltzer water

Dipping sauce for Scallion Pancakes with Seafood (page 197)

In a Dutch oven or heavy-bottomed, deep-sided pot, heat 3 to 4 inches (7.5 to 10 cm) of oil to 350°F (175°C).

Meanwhile, in a mixing bowl, toss the vegetables and perilla with 2 tablespoons of the flour and 2 tablespoons of the potato starch. In another mixing bowl, mix together the remaining 1 cup (125 g) flour, 1 cup (165 g) potato starch, and the salt, then stir in the seltzer until the mixture is like crepe or thin pancake batter. Toss in the vegetables, making sure they are well coated with the batter. (Do not let them sit; they should be fried right away.)

When the oil is hot, drop the battered vegetables slowly into the pot, working away from your body, in lacy patterns. Cook the fritters until the bottom sides are slightly browned around the edges, 2 to 3 minutes, then flip and cook the other sides until crisp, about 2 more minutes. Remove them from the oil with a slotted spoon, set on a wire rack or paper towels to cool slightly, and sprinkle with salt.

Serve the fritters warm with the dipping sauce.

KIMCHEE STEW
(*Kimchee Jigae*)

SERVES 2 TO 4

This stew is ubiquitous in Korea. It's what I had for dinner most nights. On a traditional Korean table, there's always a stew or a soup of some kind, along with myriad banchan, kimchee, and, of course, plain steamed rice. In my house, there was always either kimchee jigae or Fermented Soybean Paste Soup (opposite). Take your pick, as both are delicious.

> **TIP** *You can substitute any cut of pork for bacon or to make it vegetarian, you can omit it altogether. Use old kimchee for this recipe—the funkier the better! And as always for additional flavor, substitute Korean anchovy stock for water.*

6   ounces (175 g) bacon, cut into 1-inch
      (2.5-cm) pieces

1   cup (125 g) finely diced onion

2   cups (370 g) chopped kimchee (page 193)

2   teaspoons gochujaru (Korean dried red
      pepper flakes; see page 21)

1   tablespoon gochujang (Korean red chile
      paste; see page 21)

2   scallions, white and green parts, sliced into
      1-inch (2.5-cm) pieces

8   ounces (225 g) firm tofu, cut into 1-inch
      (2.5-cm) cubes
      Cooked white rice, for serving

In a medium stockpot, cook the bacon over medium heat until it is cooked through but not crispy, or it will taste rubbery and dry in the stew. Remove most of the bacon grease, leaving about 1 tablespoon of the grease and the bacon in the pot.

Add the onion and kimchee and sauté them until the onion is soft and translucent, 5 to 8 minutes.

Add 3 cups (720 ml) water, the gochujaru, and the gochujang. Bring to a boil and simmer for 30 minutes.

Add the scallions and tofu and cook for 10 minutes more, or until they are heated through. Serve piping hot with cooked white rice.

FERMENTED SOYBEAN PASTE SOUP
(*Doenjang Jigae*)

SERVES 4

This is the other ubiquitous soup in Korean homes! The sight of this soup bubbling away on the stove means dinner is almost ready. This is Korea's answer to miso soup. I might be biased, but I like it better. It is heftier and heartier, fortified with squash, lots of garlic, potato, and chiles. It is one of the very few Korean soups and stews that does not require umami from meat or anchovies. This should be accompanied by perfectly steamed rice and kimchee, as always, plus banchan (see pages 186 to 191), broiled fish, toasted seaweed, mung bean pancakes (page 198), or whatever you like.

6	cloves garlic
4	large dried shiitake mushrooms
1	(4-inch/10-cm) piece dried kelp
¼	cup (70 g) good-quality deongjang (Korean fermented soybean paste; see page 20)
1	cup (125 g) finely diced onion
2	cups (300 g) medium-diced Yukon gold potatoes
1½	cup (200 g) medium-dice zucchini
1	cheong-gochu (Korean green chile; see page 21) or jalapeño, thinly sliced
1	cup (50 g) sliced fresh shiitake mushrooms
8	ounces (225 g) firm tofu, cut into 1-inch (2.5-cm) cubes

Crush 2 of the garlic cloves with the back of a kitchen knife. Add them to a small pot with the dried mushrooms, kelp, and 1 quart (960 ml) water. Bring the mixture to a simmer and cook for 30 minutes. Remove all the solids, pressing out all the liquid back into the pot.

Thinly slice the remaining 4 cloves of garlic. Whisk the soybean paste into the stock, add the garlic cloves and the onion, and bring the mixture to a boil.

Simmer for 10 minutes, then add the potatoes, zucchini, cheong-gochu, fresh shiitakes, and tofu. Simmer for another 10 minutes, or until the potatoes are tender. Serve the soup bubbling hot with rice and accompaniments.

SILKEN TOFU STEW
(*Soondubu*)

SERVES 2 TO 4

This is the best use of silken tofu ever. This stew is creamy, slightly spicy, and thoroughly satisfying. Use the best-quality seafood you can, and don't limit yourself to shrimp and squid only. Cleaned clams and mussels will add another dimension. It would be best to use a traditional Korean unglazed earthenware *ttukbaegi* pot if you have one; if not, use the smallest stockpot you have.

1	tablespoon neutral oil, such as canola
¼	medium onion, diced
2	scallions, thinly sliced, white and green parts separated
2	teaspoons minced garlic
½	cup (25 g) sliced fresh shiitake mushrooms
⅓	cup (70 g) chopped kimchee (page 193)
1	cup (240 ml) Master Korean Dashi (recipe below)
2	tablespoons gochujaru (Korean dried red pepper flakes; see page 21)
2	tablespoons soy sauce
1	tablespoon myeol chi aek jeot (Korean anchovy fish sauce; see page 21)
½	cup (70 g) mixed fresh seafood, such as shrimp, squid, clams, or mussels
12	ounces (340 g) silken tofu, broken into large chunks with a spoon
1	large egg
2	cups (80 g) fresh watercress

In a small stockpot, heat the oil over medium heat. Saute the onion, white part of the scallions, garlic, mushrooms, and kimchee until fragrant, about 5 minutes.

Add the dashi, gochujaru, soy sauce, and fish sauce, bring to a simmer, then add the seafood and tofu and cook until the seafood is almost cooked through, another 5 minutes.

Crack the egg into the stew, garnish with the scallion greens and the watercress, and serve immediately.

MASTER KOREAN DASHI
(*Korean Anchovy Stock*)

MAKES 1 QUART (960 ML)

¼	cup (40 g) anchovies, cleaned (heads and guts removed)
¼	medium onion, sliced
4	large cloves garlic, crushed with the back of a kitchen knife
1	(4-inch/10-cm) piece kombu seaweed
5	dried shiitake mushrooms

In a small stockpot, combine the anchovies, onion, garlic, kombu, and shiitakes with 5 cups (1.2 L) water. Bring them just to below a boil. (Boiling will make the dashi bitter.) Simmer for 30 minutes, then strain and discard the solids, reserving the kombu for Soybean Sprout Salad banchan (see page 188), or toss it with soy sauce for ramen, if you like.

SEAWEED SOUP
(*Miyeokguk*)

SERVES 10

Also known as Birthday Soup, this is one of my all-time favorite soups. I make a big batch and eat it all week to celebrate a birthday or just to ward off a cold. It is a very comforting dish that I turn to when I am feeling out of sorts. My kids love it too; seaweed is filled with such great umami flavor that it isn't lost on children, who also like the soft, supple texture of the seaweed. However, one look at the seaweed aisle of your local Asian market will tell you that there's an amazing variety of it out there. For this dish, look for the words *ito-wakame* or *wakame*. (They are Japanese terms, and the Korean variety always comes with quotation marks around the words.) It is very important to soak it in warm water for at least twenty minutes before you use it, to soften it. Incidentally, this soup is given to women after childbirth to restore lost iron, calcium, and other vitamins. I personally ate about ten potfuls prepared by my mom and never got sick of it.

2	tablespoons extra-virgin olive oil
1	pound (455 g) beef chuck, cut into ½-inch (12-mm) cubes
10	cloves garlic, minced (about ⅓ cup)
1	ounce (28 g) dried ito-wakame or wakame seaweed, soaked in 2 cups (480 ml) warm water
2	tablespoons sesame oil
1	teaspoon mirin
1	teaspoon myeol chi aek jeot (Korean anchovy fish sauce; see page 21) or fish sauce
2	teaspoons soy sauce
2	teaspoons kosher salt
1	teaspoon freshly ground black pepper
3	scallions, white and green parts, thinly sliced
1	tablespoon sesame seeds

In a large, heavy-bottomed pot, heat the olive oil over high heat and sear the meat until it is well browned and crusted on all sides, 5 to 7 minutes.

Add the garlic and sauté it until it is fragrant, about 1½ minutes.

Drain the seaweed and add it to the pot along with the sesame oil. Cook both for about 3 minutes over medium-high heat, then add 3 quarts (2.8 L) water and the mirin, fish sauce, soy sauce, salt, and black pepper.

Bring to a boil, then reduce the heat and simmer until the meat is tender, about 1½ hours. Season to taste with more fish sauce, soy sauce, or salt. Garnish with scallions and sesame seeds and serve hot.

BIBIMBAP

WITH *vegetables* AND *eggs*

SERVES 6

This traditional Korean breakfast dish—filled with veggies and a spicy sauce and rice that keeps you on your toes—was the first thing on my mind when I was contemplating the launch of our brunch program a few years ago. We'd always been a dinner place and, after six years, adding breakfast was harder than I thought it would be. This dish would be one of the ways to distinguish ourselves. Plus, it is what I want to break my fast with. If it seems filling, consider that most things you eat for brunch make you want to crawl back into bed after eating them. It might be a challenge for some people to have a rice bowl first thing in the morning, but we Asians do it all the time! And guess what—this dish is also great at every meal. The whole sizzling stone bowl you sometimes see is a restaurant thing. Traditionally, at home, you would just take many of the previous night's leftover vegetables or banchan and place them atop a bowl of steamed rice with a spoonful of gochujang sauce, which is like Korean ketchup, and mix the whole thing up. The fried egg is just an extra bonus point. You can also add some Bulgogi (page 211), or any protein you like.

> TIP *Koreans typically use spinach, carrots, cooked soybean sprouts, mushrooms, and wild ferns for the vegetables, and I've given you my suggestions for vegetables here, but you can really use any vegetables you have or leftover banchan. Just prepare them separately, so they have different textures and flavors, and be sure to think about seasonality and color.*

FOR THE GOCHUJANG SAUCE

- ¼ cup (60 ml) gochujang (Korean red chile paste; see page 21)
- 2 tablespoons dark brown sugar
- 2 tablespoons olive oil
- 1 tablespoon sesame oil
- 2 to 3 teaspoons rice wine vinegar
- 1 to 2 teaspoons gochujaru (Korean dried red pepper flakes; see page 21)

FOR THE FINISHED DISH

- 6 cups (600 g) steamed sushi rice, kept warm
- 1 bunch kale or Swiss chard, leaves chopped into 1-inch (2.5-cm) pieces
- 2 large carrots, shredded or cut into 2 by ¼-inch (5-cm by 6-mm) matchstick strips
- 8 ounces (225 g) green beans, blanched and cut into 1-inch (2.5-cm) pieces
- 2 medium onions, thinly sliced and cooked until soft and lightly browned
- 8 ounces (225 g) fresh cremini or button mushrooms, thinly sliced and sautéed
- 6 large eggs, fried sunny-side up
  Sliced scallions, for garnish
  Sesame seeds, for garnish

Make the gochujang sauce: In a small bowl or jar, combine the gochujang, brown sugar, olive oil, sesame oil, vinegar, and gochujaru, adjusting the vinegar and gochujaru to taste. Set aside.

Once you have all the remaining ingredients at the ready, compose the dish. In a bowl, place a mound of rice and top it with the five different vegetables. Dollop the sauce around the bowl and top with a fried egg and some scallions and sesame seeds. Serve with extra sauce and encourage each diner to mix up their own bowl.

GRILLED SIRLOIN
(*Bulgogi*)

SERVES 6 TO 8

I love that we are living in a time when kimchee and bulgogi—everyone's favorite things at a Korean barbecue restaurant—are well known to most diners and food lovers. Growing up in Korea in the seventies, we had bulgogi (*bul* means "fire" and *gogi* means "meat") very rarely. It was for very special occasions. But every once in a while, we would have a pile of it on the table and I would fight over the extra sauce so that I could drown my rice in it and top the bowl with a piece of kimchee. The sweetness of the meat and sauce combined with the nicely fermented cabbage is one of those flavor combinations made in heaven! To make this a proper Korean meal, serve it with steamed rice, one of the soups in this chapter, kimchee, and at least one or two other banchan.

TIP *The easiest way to slice sirloin very thinly is to partially freeze it first.*

FOR THE MARINADE
1	cup (240 ml) soy sauce
2/3	cup (135 g) sugar
2/3	cup (85 g) grated onion
2/3	cup (120 g) grated Asian pear
2	tablespoons minced garlic
2	tablespoons sesame oil
2	teaspoons minced peeled fresh ginger
2	teaspoons freshly ground black pepper

FOR THE BULGOGI
4	pounds (1.8 kg) sirloin, sliced as thinly as possible
	Vegetable oil, for frying
1	medium onion, thinly sliced lengthwise

FOR THE FINISHED DISH
Ssam Jang (page 34)

Green or red leaf lettuce, washed and dried

Perilla (shiso) leaves, washed and dried (see Tip, page 201)

Make the marinade: In a nonreactive container, bowl, or zip-top bag, combine the soy sauce, sugar, onion, pear, garlic, sesame oil, ginger, and pepper. Add the sliced sirloin and marinate it for at least 30 minutes or refrigerate overnight.

Make the bulgogi: Heat just enough oil to coat the bottom of a grill or medium skillet over medium heat. Remove the meat from the marinade; add it to the pan and cook to your desired degree of doneness—Koreans prefer well done. Set aside. Cook or grill the onion slices in the same pan until they are soft and translucent and set them aside.

Serve the meat on a platter with the onions and small bowls of ssam jang and plates with lettuce and perilla leaves. Diners should place the perilla in a lettuce leaf, add a smear of ssam jang, then top it with the meat and onions, roll the whole thing up, and eat it with their hands.

STIR-FRIED SQUID
(*Ojingo-Bokkum*)

SERVES 6 TO 8

There are many dishes with squid in this book. I am a big fan of this creature for many reasons: On the Northeast coast, it's usually local and sustainable; it's always low in fat (so long as you don't bread and deep-fry it); and it's a good source of protein. But most importantly, it's always affordable, even when you're buying the very best quality. It's sometimes the only item that doesn't make me cringe when I stand in line at a fish market. Originally, I was going to add a simple stir-fry of cleaned squid to this book, with a little butter and salt and pepper. But then I thought about this Korean version, which is also very simple and packs a big flavor punch considering how quick it is to make. The actual cooking time is less than ten minutes, and prepping always goes faster with a glass of wine. Don't skip scoring the squid; that way it opens up and soaks up the sauce. Serve it with noodles or steamed rice.

> **TIP** *If you buy uncleaned squid, gently pull apart the body/legs from the tube. Cut the legs right below the eyes—cutting them in half if they're too large—and discard the guts. It's up to you whether you want to take the skin off; it's edible, but it also comes off easily.*

FOR THE SAUCE

2	tablespoons gochujang (Korean red chile paste; see page 21), plus extra if needed
1 1/2	tablespoons sugar, plus extra if needed
1	tablespoon gochujaru (Korean dried red pepper flakes; see page 21)
1	tablespoon soy sauce, plus extra if needed
1	tablespoon minced garlic
1	tablespoon sesame seeds
2	teaspoons sesame oil

FOR THE SQUID

2	pounds (910 g) cleaned squid
2	tablespoons neutral oil, such as canola
1/2	medium onion, thickly sliced from root to stem
1	small carrot, thinly sliced on the bias
1	cheong-gochu (Korean green chile; see page 21) or jalapeño, thinly sliced
3	scallions, whites cut into thin rings, greens into 2-inch (5-cm) strips

Make the sauce: In a small bowl, mix together the gochujang, sugar, gochujaru, soy sauce, garlic, sesame seeds, and sesame oil. Set aside.

Make the squid: Open up the tubes by running a knife from bottom to top. Clean and rinse the tubes, score them on the inside, then cut them into bite-size strips.

In a wok or a large skillet, heat 1 tablespoon of the neutral oil over high heat and cook the onion, carrot, cheong-gochu, and scallions, stirring, just until they begin to soften, 3 to 4 minutes. Remove them from the pan and set them aside in a bowl. Add 1 more tablespoon of the oil and when it begins to smoke, add the squid and stir-fry for 1 minute.

Add the sauce and vegetables back to the pan, tossing everything together, and cook until the squid is cooked through and everything is coated well in the sauce—just 2 to 3 minutes. Season to taste with sugar, soy sauce, or more gochujang if desired and serve immediately.

SPICY BEEF SOUP
(*Yukgaejang*)

SERVES 8

This is a very popular soup with taxi and truck drivers in Korea. You see it on menus at small but delicious dives, especially those on the roadside. It's meant to be eaten as a full meal, with a bowl of rice and some kimchee. My mother makes a really good version, but it turns out that she—like most places—finishes the soup with a bit of powdered flavored dashi to boost the already flavor-packed soup. This version is pure and simple, all from scratch, and tastes just as good.

TIP *The dried bracken in this dish is a type of fern sold under that name. It is easily found in Korean or large Asian markets.*

FOR THE STOCK

1	tablespoon neutral oil, such as canola
1 1/4	pounds (570 g) flank steak
1/2	medium onion, cut into large dice
5	dried anchovies, head and guts removed
3	cloves garlic, crushed with the back of a kitchen knife

FOR THE SAUCE

1 1/2	cups (35 g) dried Korean bracken
5	tablespoons gochujaru (Korean dried red pepper flakes; see page 21)
2	tablespoons minced garlic
2	tablespoons sesame oil
2	tablespoons soy sauce
1	tablespoon olive oil
1	tablespoon kosher salt
1	teaspoon freshly ground black pepper
1	large bunch spring onions or 2 bunches large scallions, halved and cut into 2-inch (5-cm) strips
1	leek, white and light green parts only, cut into 2-inch (5-cm) strips
1/3	pound (125 g) dangmyeun (sweet potato noodles)
2	large eggs

Make the stock: In a large stockpot, heat the oil over medium-high heat and sear the flank steak on all sides, 8 to 10 minutes.

Add 4 quarts (3.8 L) water to the pot and the onion, anchovies, and crushed garlic. Bring to a boil, reduce the heat to low, and simmer for 1 hour.

Make the sauce: In a small pot, cover the bracken with warm water and bring it to a boil. Cover the pot and simmer the bracken until it is fully hydrated, about 1 hour. Drain, rinse, and cut it into 2-inch (5-cm) strips; set aside.

In a small bowl, combine the gochujaru, garlic, sesame oil, soy sauce, olive oil, salt, and pepper. Add the rehydrated bracken, the spring onions, and leek, tossing to mix. Set aside.

Cook the noodles: Bring a medium pot of water to a boil and cook the noodles until they are tender, about 5 minutes. Drain them, rinse them with cold water, and cut them into 4-inch (12-cm) pieces with kitchen shears. Set them aside.

When the stock is ready, remove the flank steak and strain out and discard any other solids. Let the steak rest for 30 minutes, then slice it into thin strips, cut against the grain. Set aside.

Add the sauce with the onions and bracken to the stock and cook on a low simmer for 30 minutes. Add the thinly sliced beef, then gently crack the eggs into the pot, breaking them up with a fork to loosely scramble them into the stock. Add the cooked noodles and taste for salt and pepper.

Serve immediately with banchan (see pages 186 to 191) or kimchee and a bowl of rice.

STIR-FRIED SWEET POTATO NOODLES
(*Japchae*)

SERVES 4 TO 6

This is a traditional *janchi* (party) dish, and I usually end up making this for big groups of people because it does require a bit of time to prepare, with so many vegetables to cook separately. The *chae* in japchae means "to julienne," almost to mimic the noodles, and in the end the vegetables and noodles become a wonderfully tangled mess. But the flavors are delicious and simple—not as sweet as the Americanized fast-food version you sometimes find—and it's great for a Sunday meal. The noodles, or *dangmyeun*, are sweet potato noodles found in most Asian markets. They are quite resilient after cooking, so Koreans put them in lots of soups and stews—they are springy and fun to eat. They also work great as leftovers; just warm them up in a frying pan and watch how the noodles go from fat and cloudy when cold to slinky and glossy when they're kissed by the heat. If you have extra veggies after making this, save them for a Bibimbap (page 208) the next day. You can also use green cabbage or Swiss chard leaves instead of the spinach or arugula.

FOR THE NOODLES

6	ounces (170 g) dried dangmyeun (sweet potato noodles)
1	tablespoon sesame oil
2	teaspoons soy sauce
1	teaspoon sugar

FOR THE STIR-FRY

	Grapeseed oil
1/2	medium onion, thinly sliced
	Kosher salt
1	medium carrot, cut into 2 by 1/4-inch (5-cm by 6-mm) matchstick strips
8	ounces (225 g) fresh cremini mushrooms, stemmed and thinly sliced
1	tablespoon grated peeled fresh ginger
1	bunch spinach or arugula, stems trimmed
1	small red, yellow, or orange bell pepper, cut into 2 by 1/4-inch (5-cm by 6-mm) matchstick strips
1	tablespoon grated garlic
1	tablespoon soy sauce, plus extra if needed
1	tablespoon sugar, plus extra if needed
1	teaspoon freshly ground black pepper, plus extra if needed
2	teaspoons sesame oil, plus extra if needed
1	tablespoon sesame seeds, plus extra for garnish
3	egg yolks, beaten
2	scallions, white and green parts, thinly sliced on the bias

RECIPE FOLLOWS

Make the noodles: In a large pot of boiling water, cook the noodles until they are done according to the package directions, 5 to 7 minutes. Drain the noodles and rinse them in cold water. In a large bowl, toss them with the sesame oil, soy sauce, and sugar and set them aside.

Make the stir-fry: In a large skillet, heat a thin film of grapeseed oil over medium heat and sauté the onion until it is soft. Add a pinch of salt and add the onion to the bowl with the noodles.

Return the large skillet to the heat and cook the carrot until it is soft, about 1½ minutes, then add it to the bowl with the noodles.

Add a bit more oil to the pan, then the mushrooms and the grated ginger. Cook them until the mushrooms have released all their liquid and the pan is almost dry, then add them to the bowl with the noodles.

Add more oil to the pan and cook the leafy greens until they have wilted fully, about 2 minutes. Drain off any liquid and place the greens in a separate bowl, to catch all the leftover water they'll exude.

Working in the same skillet, add more oil and cook the bell pepper until soft, for a minute or two, and add it to the bowl with the noodles.

Squeeze the excess water from the wilted greens and add them to the bowl with the noodles. Stir in the garlic, soy sauce, sugar, black pepper, sesame oil, and sesame seeds. Taste for seasoning and add more soy sauce, sugar, black pepper, or sesame oil if necessary. Set aside.

Heat a thin film of grapeseed oil in a small skillet over medium heat and pan-fry the beaten egg yolks, flipping once, to make a thin omelet. Place the cooked eggs on a cutting board and slice them into thin strips.

Serve the noodles and vegetables garnished with the ribbons of omelet, a sprinkle of sesame seeds, and sliced scallions.

To Ben Schneider, my husband and partner, my number one fan, thank you for building my world!

To Rachel Wharton for all the laughs, your way with words, and your passion for great food—thank you!

To Hannah Kirshner, my coconspirator, recipe tester, kid-wrangler, and doer of life with many talents—thank you!

To Buj and Zach for the exquisite photos, Sarah Ryhanen of amazing Saipua Flowers, Jessie Lazar for gorgeous plate ware, and Elizabeth Goodspeed and Pam Brewer for the help on shoot days. My friends—my models who made shoot days so pleasurable and fun. Many thanks!

To all who made this book possible: Jenni Ferrari-Adler and the wonderful team at ABRAMS: Holly Dolce, Deb Wood, Michael Sand, Sarah Massey—I can't thank you enough for making this happen!

This book started ten years ago when I scribbled my first recipes on C-fold towels and slipped them into the kitchen binder. On the cover of the binder, using a sharpie, I drew a bunny rabbit holding a martini glass in one hand and a cigarette in the other. It was the Good Fork handy-dandy recipe book and there have been many who have helped me bring it to life.

Ultimate thanks to all of the Good Forking cooks who have come through this tiny kitchen and have made a difference: Rostislav Kemelman, Patty Gentry, David Lewis, Sam Filloramo, Lorraine Bashian, Sawako Okochi, Marcelo Palacios, Anna Kalthoff, Yuan Tang, Ben Martin, Dan Wolinsky, Cathy Charnock, Rigo Vazquez, Jessica "Jecala" Binkley, Frank Pagano, Caroline "Carla" Schiff, Lupin Mindlin, Alia Truett, Yong Sup Shin, Tim Gardner, Trevor Safrani, Demetrius Donahue, Ryan Coleman, Ricardo "Primo" Asitimbay, Justin Augustus, Santa Wolanczyk, Michael "Ajeossi" Stokes, Lauren O'Conner, Sarah Evans, Kara Lewis, Jared Levin, Sasha Coulter, Paul Baker, Jess Nizar, Jose Recinos, and of course the Flores family, Alex and Daniel. Thank you.

To Meg Bouchard, who came in for dinner and stayed for ten years, and to the rest of the amazing servers who have become parts of our family and who represent our passion for food on a nightly basis—a thousand thanks!

Last but not least, thank you to all of the volunteers who helped during Hurricane Sandy recovery, to all who gave to The Good Fork along the way, to all of the interns who helped fold dumplings and peel onions. And, of course, a deep and sincere thank you to all of the wonderful customers who have time and again passed their hard earned shekels across the table in return for some good food and a nice place to eat it. And finally a shout out to Red Hook for giving The Good Fork its only possible home.

Editor: Holly Dolce
Designer: Deb Wood
Production Manager: True Sims

Library of Congress Control Number:
2015955678

ISBN: 978-1-4197-2233-2

Printed and bound in China
10 9 8 7 6 5 4 3 2 1

Abrams books are available at special
discounts when purchased in quantity for
premiums and promotions as well as fundrais-
ing or educational use. Special editions can
also be created to specification. For details,
contact specialsales@abramsbooks.com or
the address below.

ABRAMS
The Art of Books

115 West 18th Street
New York, NY 10011
www.abramsbooks.com